A Diary of the Russian Revolution

A Diary of the Russian Revolution

Edited and Annotated by

David S. Foglesong

Bloomington, Indiana, 2022

© 2022 by David S. Foglesong. All rights reserved.
Cover design by Tracey Theriault.
Cover photo courtesy of Lawrence Houghteling.

Technical Editor: Anne Marie Watkins

ISBN 978-0-89357-510-6

Library of Congress Cataloging-in-Publication Data

Names: Houghteling, James L., Jr. (James Lawrence), 1883-1962. | Foglesong, David S., editor.
Title: A diary of the Russian Revolution / edited and annotated by David S. Foglesong.
Description: Bloomington, Indiana : Slavica Publishers, 2022. | Series: Americans in Revolutionary Russia; vol. 15 | Includes bibliographical references and index. | Summary: "Diary of a special attaché to the US embassy in Russia that details the dramatic events he witnessed and comments he heard from Russian and foreign observers"-- Provided by publisher.
Identifiers: LCCN 2021050763 | ISBN 9780893575106 (paperback)
Subjects: LCSH: Houghteling, James L., Jr. (James Lawrence), 1883-1962--Diaries. | Soviet Union--History--Revolution, 1917-1921--Personal narratives, American. | Saint Petersburg (Russia)--Description and travel.
Classification: LCC DK265.7 .H7 2022 | DDC 947.084/1--dc23/eng/20211026
LC record available at https://lccn.loc.gov/2021050763

Slavica Publishers
Indiana University
1430 N. Willis Drive
Bloomington, IN 47404-2146
USA

[Tel.] 1-812-856-4186
[Toll-free] 1-877-SLAVICA
[Fax] 1-812-856-4187
[Email] slavica@indiana.edu
[www] https://slavica.indiana.edu

Contents

David S. Foglesong

    Editor's Introduction vii

A Diary of the Russian Revolution

Preface 5

Introduction 7

I. Petrograd in War Time 11

II. Rumblings 19

III. The Lull 29

IV. The Revolt 39

V. The News Bulletins of the Revolution 48

VI. The New Order Replaces the Old 63

VII. Reconstruction 78

VIII. Order or Chaos? 86

IX. The Turn Toward Order 91

Index 101

Editor's Introduction
David S. Foglesong

The Russian revolutions of 1917 were among the most significant events of the twentieth century. They profoundly influenced many developments in the following decades, not only in Russia but also around the world. The overthrow of the Romanov monarchy in February 1917 affected the United States' decision to declare war against Germany in April and altered the course of the First World War. The Bolshevik-led seizure of power in October 1917 sparked an ideological conflict between socialist dictatorships and liberal capitalism that would last more than seventy years.[1] If the Russian revolutions had not happened, the history of the twentieth century would have been dramatically different.

In the twenty-first century, it continues to be important to understand how Americans perceived and misperceived the Russian revolutions at the time for at least two reasons. First, if Americans had better understood developments in revolutionary Russia, the United States might have pursued wiser, more effective policies toward Russia. Second, some of the oversimplifications, illusions, and misconceptions of Americans in 1917 such as the notion that Russians were destined to follow the example of the United States have continued to affect US policies in the post-Cold War world.

The most valuable records of American perceptions and misperceptions that have been preserved include the diaries of two US diplomats: Joshua Butler Wright, the counselor at the US embassy in Petrograd, and James L. Houghteling, Jr., a special attaché to the embassy.[2] Examining the day-by-day notes of the diplomats makes it possible to see how they formed and affirmed their beliefs.

---

[1] Since the Julian calendar in use in Russia was thirteen days behind the Gregorian calendar, the revolutions occurred in March and November according to the calendar in the United States.

[2] Joshua Butler Wright's diaries have been deposited at the Seeley G. Mudd Manuscript Library, Princeton University, and extracts have been published in William Allison, ed., *Witness to Revolution: The Russian Revolution Diary and Letters of J. Butler Wright* (Westport, CT: Praeger, 2002).

Since Houghteling has received little attention from historians[3] and his personal papers were not preserved, his diary offers a unique record of his observations and thoughts. A native of Chicago from a family of bankers, Houghteling served as a special attaché to the American embassy in Petrograd in the first few months of 1917. The thirty-three-year-old assisted with providing aid to German and Austro-Hungarian prisoners of war in Russia, a task the United States undertook as a neutral in the European war. From January 18 to April 8, he recorded in a diary what he saw in Petrograd, in Moscow, and on the train between the cities, as well as what he heard from American colleagues and Russian acquaintances.

After returning to the United States, Houghteling married Laura Delano in May 1917, then had his diary published early in 1918. The diary did not have great impact on American public thinking about Russia. It received only a few short reviews, which were at best polite and at worst sharply critical.[4] One kind reviewer praised the book's "genuine effectiveness and interest."[5] Less indulgent reviewers criticized the brevity of Houghteling's depiction of the crucial days of revolt, his reliance on "second-hand information," and his alleged pro-business bias.[6] However, the diary presents vivid accounts of some key events in revolutionary Russia and it reveals who influenced Houghteling's perspective.

Houghteling did not learn much Russian during his brief time in Russia. In one moment of exasperation at the start of his service, on January 21, he asked: "why doesn't any one speak anything beside Russian?" Near the end of his tour of duty, Houghteling understood enough Russian to recognize that fellow passengers on a train were talking about America and Americans, but he could engage in conversation only with those who spoke French or German.[7]

As a result, Houghteling depended heavily on information, rumors, speculation, and predictions from fellow Americans, Britons, and Russians who could speak foreign languages. Houghteling was influenced especially strongly by Samuel Harper, a professor from the University of Chicago whom Houghteling thanked in his preface for helping him to understand Russian institutions, politics, and customs. Other figures who shaped Houghteling's views included Joshua Butler Wright; British journalist Harold Williams and his wife Ariadna Tyrkova-Williams; wealthy Russian women who hosted parties that Houghteling attended; and Aleksandr Ivanovich Guchkov, a

---

[3] Two exceptions are Norman Saul, *War and Revolution: The United States and Russia, 1914–1921* (Lawrence: University Press of Kansas, 2001), 82–83; and Helen Rappaport, *Caught in the Revolution: Petrograd, Russia, 1917—A World on the Edge* (New York: St. Martin's Press, 2016).

[4] James L. Houghteling, Jr., *A Diary of the Russian Revolution* (New York: Dodd, Mead, 1918).

[5] *The Dial*, March 28, 1918, 301.

[6] "The Problem in Russia: A Three Months' Record of Revolutionary Events," *Boston Evening Transcript*, April 3, 1918, 6; *New Republic*, April 20, 1918, 306.

[7] See the diary entry for March 23, p. 89.

conservative politician who became the first minister of war in the Provisional Government formed after the collapse of the Romanov autocracy.

Tyrkova-Williams, a prominent feminist, was a leader of the Kadet (Constitutional Democrat) party and Samuel Harper had close ties to the Kadets, including Paul Miliukov, a professor of law who became the first foreign minister in the Provisional Government. Perhaps in part because of such connections, Houghteling tended to view developments in Russia through a Kadet-like framework, including the Kadet conception of the transcendence of class interests.[8] Thus, one of the most striking features of the book is how frequently Houghteling praises unselfishness and altruism virtues that are contrasted explicitly to "the crude selfishness of the [tsarist] bureaucracy" and implicitly to working class radicalism. In the very first line of his introduction, Houghteling stressed how he had been "tremendously impressed by the ardent sentimental love which all classes of people show for their broad-stretching fatherland." That "enthusiastic love," he continued, explained "the great phenomenon of the Russian Revolution of this year 1917: the entire lack of selfish ambitions." That assumption would make it difficult to have a sympathetic understanding of peasants' yearning to seize land from noble owners, workers' desires to take control of factories, and soldiers' longing for an end to the war.

Like Houghteling, many Russian liberals, including Tyrkova-Williams, felt that Russians in Petrograd in March 1917 experienced a miraculous rebirth that purified them of selfishness and fostered a new sense of community or brotherhood. Yet Tyrkova-Williams soon concluded that the supposed "unity was fictitious," that the belief that all the partitions between people had disappeared was an illusion.[9] Americans like Houghteling, in contrast, persisted in that belief about the revolution.

Houghteling knew that workers had been key actors in the overthrow of the tsarist autocracy and that some of them militantly asserted themselves at factories. On March 13, he recorded: "Petrograd is absolutely in the hands of the uprisen soldiers and workmen." Three days later, he noted, "We were much impressed to see a great red flag waving over the Winter Palace…" Although Houghteling may not have understood fully the meanings of red flags, he clearly grasped the implications of a story he heard of an American who owned a manufacturing plant in Petrograd, and whose factory employees suddenly refused to work full-time. When the American owner fired the workers, Houghteling noted, "they defied him and would not leave the building." Houghteling also knew that many workers expressed enthusiasm for socialism. On March 25, watching the massive Liberty Parade, Houghteling witnessed how a

---

[8] On Kadet ideas of *nadklassnost'*, see William G. Rosenberg, *Liberals in the Russian Revolution: The Constitutional Democratic Party, 1917–1921* (Princeton, NJ: Princeton University Press, 1974), esp. 83–92.

[9] Ariadna Tyrkova-Williams, *From Liberty to Brest-Litovsk: The First Year of the Russian Revolution* (London: Macmillan, 1919), 10–13.

"section of red socialists ... suddenly struck up a hymn, and every one in the crowd immediately joined soldiers, marchers and spectators."

Influenced by what he learned from wealthy Russians at a tea party, Houghteling expressed concern about socialists' "preponderance among the workingmen in Petrograd," and recorded that "the problem is to put them back in their places without bloodshed." Thus, he began to consider the need for a strong military leader to restore order and to think that "perhaps more blood must be shed."[10] On April 1, Houghteling reported being highly impressed by seeing General Lavr Korniloff riding in the midst of "a stunning group of staff officers" and receiving smart salutes from soldiers on the sidewalks. He went on to reflect: "If these soldiers will obey, there will be order in the city and an end of the spirit of superciliousness on the part of the workingmen..."[11]

Yet on the whole, Houghteling refused to allow the working class radicalism he saw and heard to dim his optimism. On March 20, after listening to "a timorous American" spread "pessimistic rumors," including tales that workers were refusing to go back to work at the munitions factories, Houghteling insisted on maintaining faith in Russia: "If one believes some of these faint-hearts, she is about done for. We think that she is just beginning."

Houghteling similarly set aside ominous rumors and evidence of antiwar sentiment among soldiers. With his own eyes, Houghteling, on March 12, "watched officers trying vainly to make a battalion fall in"; some of the soldiers instead gave away their guns and walked away. Even when an officer drew his revolver and pointed it at the soldiers, many of them just shrugged their shoulders. Houghteling knew that not only in Petrograd, but also at the front, many soldiers were deserting, in part from a desire to return to their home villages to participate in the division of seized lands of nobles. Yet, like Ambassador David Francis and almost all other diplomats present at a meeting at the US embassy on March 16, Houghteling refused to accept one American's pessimistic forecast that "the revolution will take all the starch out of the troops at the front, and that we can no longer figure Russia as a factor in the war." Instead he focused on indications that supported what he wanted to believe. "Anti-war talk isn't popular," Houghteling concluded after seeing soldiers, officers, students, and civilians in his train carriage denounce "an untidy socialist" who argued against the war. Seeing many soldiers resume saluting their officers in Moscow, he observed on March 25: "This is a good sign." Perhaps most importantly, Houghteling pointed to a photograph that he placed as a frontispiece to his book: it showed soldiers marching

---

[10] From diary entries for March 25, p. 91, and March 27, p. 94.

[11] Houghteling thus foreshadowed the later hopes of American diplomats and officials that Kornilov would use troops from the front to suppress radicalism in the capital. See David S. Foglesong, *America's Secret War Against Bolshevism: U.S. Intervention in the Russian Civil War, 1917–1920* (Chapel Hill: The University of North Carolina Press, 1995), 54–55.

in Petrograd on April 1, 1917, carrying a banner that declared: "In the Name of Liberty, War Against Germanism to Full Victory."

As the United States hesitantly moved toward entering the war against Germany in March 1917, Americans both in Petrograd and at home knew that their country was not ready to fight. If Russia left the war before enough doughboys could be trained, outfitted, and sent to France, Germany would be able to transfer divisions from the Eastern Front and perhaps defeat the Allies on the Western Front. Many Americans, including Houghteling, therefore wanted very badly to believe that the removal of the allegedly pro-German Empress Aleksandra, the ouster of bureaucrats who favored peace, and the establishment of a popular representative government would lead Russia not only to stay in the war, but to wage it more enthusiastically and effectively than before.[12] Wishful thinking thus contributed to the widespread interpretation of the revolution against the autocracy as a triumph of American-style liberty.[13]

Houghteling shared that view. After seeing a news bulletin declaring that people had a right to know what was happening, Houghteling proclaimed it "a new charter of liberty for Russia." After a long lunch on March 20 with Professor Boris Bakhmeteff (who would soon be sent as ambassador to Washington), Houghteling enthusiastically commented on how the Provisional Government's deep interest in relations with America and its desire to "open every possible facility for American trade" offered great promise that "Free Russia" would "leap ahead with tremendous strides." The next day, after meeting with the new minister of public enlightenment, Houghteling noted how the Provisional Government planned to expand primary schooling "to make the people fit for self-government" and to model the educational system on the American example. At the end of March, after lunching with the Wrights, Houghteling observed that the Provisional Government more generally considered "the United States its model and its best friend." All of this fueled Houghteling's faith in the Americanization and democratization of Russia, which he maintained even as he prepared his diary for publication in November 1917. The revolution against the tsarist autocracy, he wrote in his introduction to the book, stemmed from "the same sort of exalted patriotism that inspired the fathers of the American nation in our Revolution."

This intense faith led logically to the belief that the Bolsheviks and other radical socialists who led the overthrow of the Provisional Government were not authentically

---

[12] Houghteling noted on February 20 that all in the Russian army believed Tsarina Aleksandra was "sending news to the Germans." On March 1, after calling upon the wife of a rich merchant, he recorded that "no one in Russia, except the desperately seared bureaucracy, wants a separate peace."

[13] For further discussion, see David S. Foglesong, *The American Mission and the "Evil Empire": The Crusade for a "Free Russia" Since 1881* (New York: Cambridge University Press, 2007), 50–52.

Russian. Like the treasonous tsarist bureaucrats earlier, they were actually agents of German intrigue, driven by "greed for the gold of the enemy," according to Houghteling.[14] That common notion, which continues to be expressed in the twenty-first century, was misleading.[15] Although the Bolsheviks received funds from Germany, the Kaiser did not direct the actions of the Bolsheviks. After they took power, they sought to promote a socialist revolution in Germany more ardently than anywhere else. Yet Houghteling was emphatic that "the Bolsheviki and extremist agitators are not blood-children of the Russian Revolution," as he declared in the introduction. A similar view of the Bolsheviks as unrepresentative of the will of the Russian people strongly influenced US policy toward the new Soviet government, which Washington refused to recognize until 1933.

As Houghteling's diary indicates, American ideas about revolutionary Russia were not merely projected onto the Russian screen by ignorant Americans in the distant United States, but also developed on the ground in interaction with Russians in Petrograd in 1917. Some of the key themes would reverberate in American-Russian relations for many decades to come, especially the influence of Westernized, English-speaking Russian elites on American notions and the blaming of evil, sinister figures for obstructing the fulfillment of Russia's natural destiny to emulate the example of the United States.

---

[14] See the entry for March 15, p. 68, and Houghteling's introduction.

[15] See Sean McMeekin, *The Russian Revolution: A New History* (New York: Basic Books, 2017).

A DIARY OF THE RUSSIAN REVOLUTION

BY

JAMES L. HOUGHTELING, JR.

With Illustrations

NEW YORK
DODD, MEAD AND COMPANY
1918

Copyright, 1918,
BY DODD, MEAD AND COMPANY, INC.

**TO
L. D. H.**

**FOR WHOM THESE CHRONICLES WERE KEPT
BUT WHO IS MENTIONED IN THEM ONLY ONCE**

Preface

This story of the Russian Revolution of March 1917 is based partly on the actual experiences of an eyewitness, partly on facts which stand of record or are common knowledge in Petrograd and Moscow, and partly on hearsay and rumour. I realise fully that information of the latter class, as, for instance, the unsupported testimony of persons whom I have only felt at liberty to designate by their initials, is a weak foundation for a historical structure. But I beg leave to point out that such testimony is in no place used as foundation, but only as the ornamental scroll-work of the façade. It is interesting to know what clever and well-informed Russians were saying and thinking in the most crucial epoch of their country's history. The men of ability who so quickly adopted this almost accidental revolution and guided it, believed the situation to be approximately what these stories and rumours depict.

I have included a few happenings which may appear to some to be too personal and therefore unnecessary, but their purpose is to show the conditions of life in a war-ridden country.

To those Americans in Russia who may be surprised to have their names "called right out in meeting," without dashes or other subterfuge, I offer apologies, feeling sure that these friends will accept them. The experiences are theirs as much as mine and my highest hope is that they may think I have drawn the picture faithfully.

I owe to the Hon. David R. Francis, American Ambassador to Russia,[1] a debt of gratitude which I gladly acknowledge; also to the Hon. Maddin Summers, American Consul at Moscow; and to the embassy and consulate staffs.

I wish to offer sincere thanks, in this place, to Professor Samuel N. Harper of the University of Chicago for the ground-outline he has given me of Russian institutions, politics and customs, which has enabled me in a greater measure to grasp the significance of what I saw and heard.

James L. Houghteling, Jr.
November 25, 1917.

---

[1] For David R. Francis's account as American ambassador to Russia during the revolution, see *Russia from the American Embassy* (Bloomington, IN: Slavica, 2019).

Introduction

A person who has spent even a few months in Russia cannot but be tremendously impressed by the ardent sentimental love which all classes of people show for their broad-stretching fatherland. Ties of family and of friendship do not seem to bind as fast as do the bonds of endless enthusiasm for "Holy Russia."

There is an irresistible appeal in its undulating flatness and fertility, in its dazzling winter whiteness, in the sense that for thousands and thousands of versts there stretches always Russia, easy-going, kindly Russia, full of impractical, religious, likeable people.

This enthusiastic love explains the great phenomenon of the Russian Revolution of this year 1917: the entire lack of selfish ambitions.

Through good-nature and indifference, the Russians had let themselves be misgoverned for a hundred years after all other great peoples had begun to reform their governments. A clique of grand-dukes, lordlings and politicians, up to the minute in every refinement of robbery, bribery and maladministration, had fastened itself upon the public treasury and the ministerial payrolls, taking cynical advantage of the confusing and obscuring bureaucratic system of "chins" or graduated civil ranks. These corrupt obstructionists had succeeded in dominating every Tsar and in nullifying every reform and concession which the crusading minority had been able to win, up to the very day of the Revolution.

That there were reforms at all was due to certain chivalrous elements of the population who from altruistic motives carried on a stubborn war against the old system. These groups were the "intelligentsia," the socialists and the terrorists,   subdivisions frequently overlapping. They lived lives of devotion to Russia and to their own plans of reform. They knew no sordid impulses within themselves and were revolted by the crude selfishness of the bureaucracy.

They won two great victories: first, in the reforms of Alexander II, the freeing of the serfs, the division of lands, and the establishment of the Zemstvos; and second, in the institution of the Imperial Duma as a climax of the revolution of 1905 1906. During the rest of the last sixty years they watched reaction triumph and had not the organised backing to defeat it, nor the ability to marshal a successful revolution. The Great War awakened and organised the people. The corrupt autocratic system was swamped from the outset, and only the unselfish energies of the alert liberal minority saved Russia from a disgraceful collapse. The Zemstvos   representative assemblies of the landed gentry and richer peasants in each of the "governments" into which Russia is divided suddenly threw off the powerlessness which the bureaucracy had imposed upon them and through their Union became the vitalising force of the war-ridden country. They cared for the wounded and fed and clothed all the armies in the field.[1] They directed and strengthened the peasant co-operative societies and thus reached out into almost every village of the fatherland.

Capitalists and toilers joined hands a second time in the War Industry Committee, composed of public-spirited merchants, manufacturers and labor leaders from all parts of the empire. They took over bodily the production and purchase of munitions and began putting Russia back on an efficient military footing after the calamitous retreat out of Poland.

These patriotic organisations were wrapped up in winning the war and tried to work with the bureaucracy. But their efficiency and popularity were regarded by the latter with suspicion and fear. The contrast was not to the advantage of the old system and the people were being educated to expect better things, which the bureaucracy had neither the inclination nor the ability to supply. Instead they did two things. They hampered patriotic endeavour in every way they could; and they tried to stop the war. The interference with the meetings of the Zemstvo Union and the arrest of the Labor Members of the War Industry Committee were stupid and brutal blows at the success of their own armies. The "separate-peace" machinations of the Tsar, Sturmer, Rasputin and Protopopoff were awkward attempts to save the old system from collapse by sacrificing the Russian people and their allies. The patriots survived all these attacks, and the reaction against the perpetrators had a tremendous momentum.

It is hardly fair to have gone so far in reviewing the unselfish patriotic forces in the Russian state without mentioning the turbulent minority in the Duma, hampered almost hopelessly by the ever-impending veto of the Council of Empire, by the overruling power of the Tsar and by the crushingly limited electoral franchise of its own body. Of the parties of Opposition, the most important were the Constitutional Democrats, the Social Democrats and the Laborites or Social Revolutionaries. There was seldom peace or agreement among these parties, but their principal aim was held in common, to free Russia from the curse of the selfish bureaucracy. Membership in any of them was an antidote to ambition, for all recognised that their leaders stood much nearer to the famous casemates of the Peter-and-Paul Fortress than they did to real nation-wide power and influence. Men like Alexander Feodorovich Kerensky or Pavel Nikolaievich Miliukoff spent their energies freely and risked life and liberty with no other motive than a true love of humanity and a burning passion of devotion for Russia.

---

[1] Footnote in original: See report of the Russian Union of Zemstvos, published in January, 1916, by its London Committee, Bank Building, Kingsway, W. C., London.

Suddenly the Revolution of March 12 came, and Russia found all her most devoted children on one side. Against the Imperial Family, the old guard of the bureaucracy, and the police, were lined up the Zemstvo nobility and gentry and their peasant collaborators, the business people, the bourgeoisie, the vast masses of the workingmen, the ablest generals in the field, and the entire army with many of its officers. Even some members of the court and one or two of the Romanoffs believed a revolution unavoidable and favoured it. Selfishness, corruption and incompetence clashed for a moment against the awakened demand for freedom, justice and humanity and then were bowled over and swept away before the advance of the reborn nation.

The methods of the old regime were accursed. The selfishness of the autocracy had its reflex in the same sort of exalted patriotism that inspired the fathers of the American nation in our Revolution. By common consent the best men in Russia were thrust into office, regardless of political differences, to form the great First Ministry. Not until the return of the Siberians and the exiles, who were untouched by the exaltation of the Revolution, did false ambition, class hatred, treason to Russia and greed for the gold of the enemy become prominent factors of the situation. The Bolsheviki and extremist agitators are not blood-children of the Russian Revolution.

The century-long work of liberation was consummated in five days. The century-long work of building up the structure of a modern system of liberty, restrained and accommodated to the welfare of an ever-increasing majority and to the rights of all, cannot be accomplished so quickly. But no one who has caught the spirit of the Revolution can doubt that the up-building of such a system will be duly finished, despite intervening disturbances, generously, wisely and patriotically.

Chapter I
Petrograd in War Time

January 18, 1917. En route from Stockholm to Petrograd. At noon we reached Haparanda and the Swedish frontier. Just before, we were treated to a most beautiful "sun-rise" effect. The sun had been up for two hours but hung low in the south, about twenty degrees above the horizon. Long low snow-islands of clouds lined the southern heavens; the sun, instead of rising across these cloud-bars as a normal rising sun would, slid sideward between them. The colors were magnificent, the whole effect very thrilling.

We were within fifteen miles of the Arctic Circle and it was moderately cold, about twenty below zero, Fahrenheit.

At Haparanda we passed laboriously through the Swedish customs. The laws about taking food, shoes, etc., out of the country are as strenuous as those governing imports.

After a frigid drive across the river to an island, we were admitted by a sort of toll-gate to the Russian Empire. Beyond the gate were a few rough wooden houses, including custom-house, warehouses, and barracks; also an enclosure with a high paling that might have been a place of detention. The Swedish sleigh-driver left us and our hand-luggage on the hard-packed snow of the little square and a Russian soldier with a *bashlik* tied tightly around his head motioned us into the custom-house. Here we were treated with great courtesy by an officer who spoke English. The examination was far from rigorous but everyone was obliged to answer an elaborate questionnaire. Then we were kept shut up for an hour or more in a packed waiting-room; we talked with a Roumanian dressed in the uniform of a captain of the French army, who was hastening home to help stop the Roumanian retreat, and with one or two Russian officers. Most of the travellers crowded into a dirty little restaurant and drank tea out of glasses.

It was in this custom-house a short time ago that a courier, having a perfectly correct passport and *laissez passer* from the Russian legation in Stockholm, was detained. Everything seemed normal but the commandant, who has been here a long time and has developed a great nose for spies, was suspicious. Despite threats from the courier that it meant ruin to the commandant's military career, the latter ordered the pouches opened, and found therein several thousand pasteboard matchboxes, each containing a couple of layers of matches and under them, tightly-folded pamphlets of a revolutionary pro-German nature addressed to the peasants of Russia. The courier was, naturally, taken out and shot. What a futile errand to pay for with a man's life!

Another cold drive across the river toward the hilly Finland shore. The crispness of the air and the slanting sunlight on the snow were most exhilarating. The wooded hills, the gilded bulb-domes of the Russian church in the village of Torneo and the long caravans of freight sledges tugging across snow-covered ice made an unforgettable picture. At the Torneo station we went through the usual confused checking of baggage and just as darkness fell Bailey and I found ourselves ensconced in a cramped compartment on the train of the Finnish National R. R. We started south only two hours late.

Friday, January 19. We travelled all day through Finland. In neatness, whiteness and woodiness it is much like Sweden but less rugged. We have not seen any really good stands of timber, but I suppose this is natural along the right-of-way of a trunk-line railway.

We passed the Finnish-Russian Customs with the usual formalities at Bieloostroff, and reached Petrograd at midnight. Armour, Johnson and a courier met us at the Finland Station. Outside, we found that the automobile they had hired had, in characteristic Russian fashion, gotten tired and gone home; so we had the long cold drive to the hotel in a sleigh. I drew two small rooms, a tiny bedroom and a fair-sized sitting-room. Dark walls, torn paper, drab furniture! The halls of this hotel smell like a third-class boarding house in Chicago.

Saturday, January 20. I went at 11:30 to call at our Embassy. The drive by the Winter Palace, the Hermitage, the Quays, the Marsovo Pole, the Summer Garden and the Liteiny made a great impression. But what an untidy town! The buildings are of such a discouraged color; perhaps in the sunlight they will look better but today is overcast. The unattractive war-loan posters are stuck about badly over everything, be it government office building or palace; and firewood is piled in full view all over town. The Marsovo Pole (Field of Mars) looks like a wood-yard.

Soldiers are drilling everywhere, on the Palace Square, on the Quays, in the side-streets. In the middle of the Marsovo Pole, surrounded by marching infantry, skirmishing machine-gun squads, and overshadowing fire-woods, two sections of field artillery are doing mounted drill, a welcome sight to an expatriated artillery-man. I was tempted to abandon my *ivoshchik* and spend my morning "reviewing" them.

The Embassy stands on a fine broad street, the Fourstadskaya, but is a disappointing two-story affair without dignity of façade, squeezed into the middle of a block with a big apartment building on one side and another modest residence on the other. Above its low roof an American flag hung at half-mast (for Admiral Dewey).

The Embassy staff were most cordial. I had a session, including luncheon, with the Ambassador and told him the reasons of my coming. He was very definite in his suggestions, and greatly impressed me by his grasp of the Russian situation and by the largeness of his views.

In the evening I dined at the hotel and was joined by ———. I went afterwards to his palatial suite for a wee drappie; we foreigners aren't as dry as the rest of Russia. ——— told me that an official in the Foreign Office had informed him that Russia was not worrying about the Roumanian situation; she has been warned by her allies that they intend to make a big push in the spring and end the war next fall, so she is bending every effort to get her house in order preparatory to doing her share. I don't know what he means by "getting her house in order."

Sunday, January 21. Went to 34 Fourstadskaya at 11 with Bailey; there we picked up Rumchevich the door-man to act as interpreter and started out to look for apartments. A handy interpreter! He speaks only Russian and German, and in this town one dare not speak the latter above a whisper. The Kaiser once said that German is a tongue which must be spoken loud from the chest, and I believe him; at least my attempts to whisper it were not very successful. We saw only one apartment and that was impossible. The bedroom and study were nice, but they were separated by a salon crammed full of heavy, inartistic Russian furniture, and the man who owned the apartment would only rent the three rooms together for 400 roubles a month.

I thought Graham Taylor might arrive today, so after leaving Bailey at the hotel I walked the length of the Nevsky to the Nikolaieff station. What a conglomeration of a street the Nevsky is! The curved colonnades of the Kazan Cathedral are stunning but in the next block one comes face to face with the atrocious city hall. The open square at the Anitchkoff and that palace itself are worthy of Paris, but across the street is a hodge-podge of straggly forlorn business buildings, much disfigured by ugly signs. It is not a creditable main street for the capital of 180,000,000 souls.

And why doesn't anyone speak anything beside Russian? At the Nikolaieff there was no one to be found to tell me about trains from Moscow and I wandered about mournfully like a lost soul. Luckily Graham didn't come, for if he had, I should probably have missed him.

Monday, January 22. To the office about ten. It's hard to get started in the morning when one has to labor with the hotel servants to make them understand one's simplest wants and then to wait interminably for service. The hotels are awfully short of even *moujik* "help," and if I get an answer to my bell in less than a half-hour, I'm proud of myself all day.

At noon Norman Armour of our Embassy took some of us newly-arrived Americans over to look at the Demidoff house on the Sergievskaya. The United States has an option on it, furnished, for an Embassy. It has seventy rooms including state reception-rooms, banquet-rooms, a ballroom, a stunning conservatory where the Demidoffs are said to have gypsy dancers perform when they give a ball, two beautiful suites of apartments for the ambassador and the counsellor, a lot of smaller suites which could be used for secretaries, and all sorts of rooms for a chancery.

We lunched with Armour at his apartment on the Liteiny, Sands and Miles being the other guests. The difficulties of living comfortably were discussed at length; all present except Armour are hunting better quarters and are having no luck at all.

Tuesday, January 23. At four this afternoon I went exploring. I had heard of an apartment over on the Bolshoy Prospekt belonging to an erstwhile secretary of the erstwhile German Embassy; but there are two Bolshoy Prospekts, widely separated on different islands, one on the Kammeny Ostroff and the other on the Vassili Ostroff, and my informant failed to tell me on which one to look for this apartment building. I started along the Quays and across the Troitsky Bridge, pausing a few moments to study the old Fortress of Peter and Paul (the needle-pointed spire of its church is the fairest thing in Petrograd); then around by the People's House of Nikolas II, a big recreation building, and into a labyrinth of back streets. Soon I reached the Bolshoy Prospekt and its shoddiness convinced me that the other one must be that for which I was looking, for not even a German secretary would live on this Second-Avenue-like thoroughfare. I felt too weak on Russian for either sleigh or street-cars, so I trudged on and presently came out of the congested district and crossed the Little Neva to the scholastic shores of the Vassili Ostroff. I had been two hours on foot and decided it was too late for any more flat-hunting. Therefore I skirted the Bourse and the Museums to the Bourse Bridge, thence to the Admiralty Quay, and across the Palace Square to the Morskaya and home. It was my first tour of the city, which after all has many points of interest and beauty.

Bailey and I dined together and went to a movie. I can already read a few words of the legends between the pictures.

Wednesday, January 24. I lunched with the Wrights told me that a revolution is much talked about in private and that some people here think it may come soon.

In the evening I went to the Imperial Ballet at the Marinsky Theatre. The ballet was *Paxita*, a Spanish affair, not one of the best, but very well done, of course. Between the acts we admired the sentinels at the door of the Imperial Box. They faced each other and stood like statues, a most blasé smirk on their nubbly Russian countenances. At fixed intervals the flicker of an eyelid of the senior would set them off on a stiff marionettish manual-of-arms drill lasting about three minutes. Heads were snapped to right and left, rifles ported, presented, shouldered, all in staccato time but with an air of utmost boredom. The Imperial Box was occupied by officers of the suite of the Crown-Prince of Roumania; who rumor says is up here courting, trying to get Tatiana, but Olga must go first.

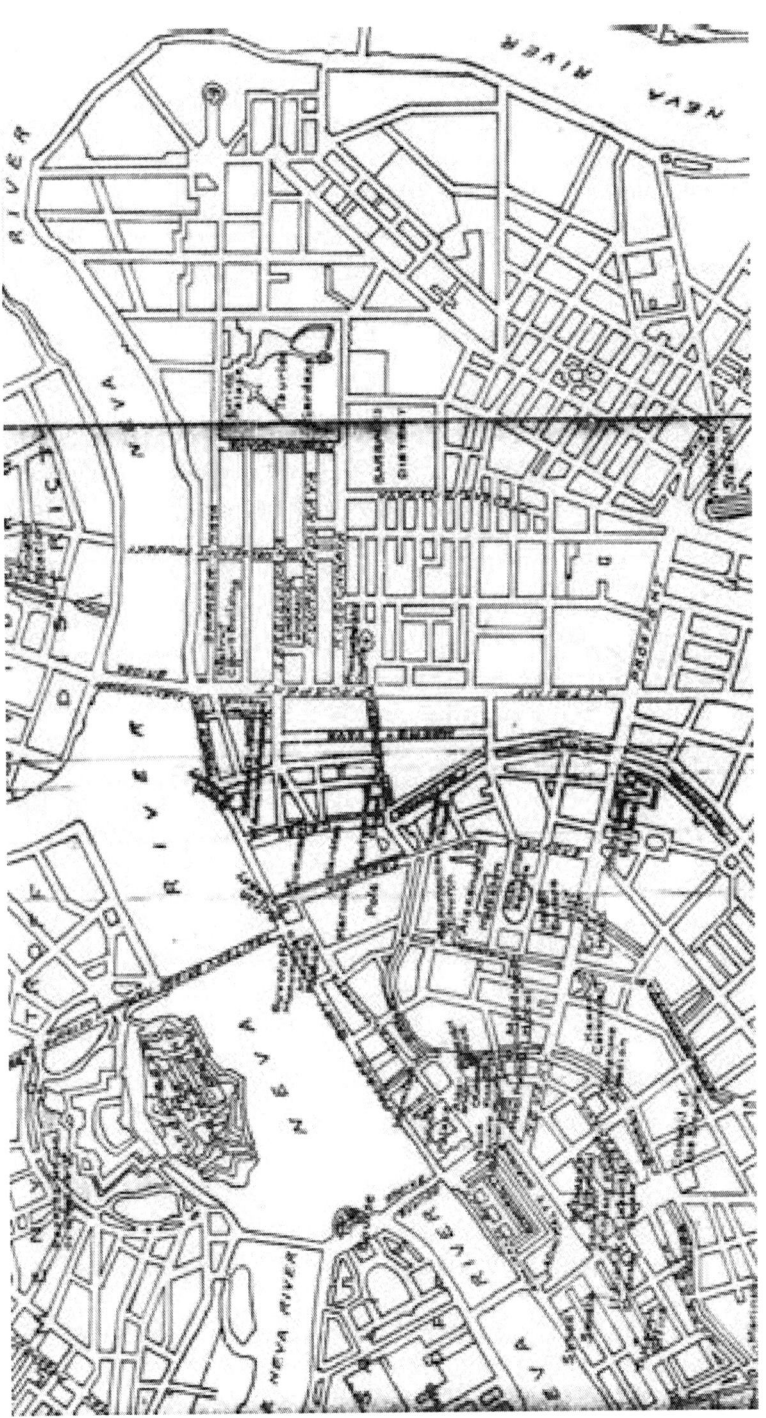

Figure 1. The central district of Petrograd.

Thursday, January 25. I have found a solution for the perplexing problem of talking to the servants in this hotel. The chambermaid is an amusing old dame from the Baltic Provinces, as quick as a steel trap, and talks German fluently. By much gesticulation and pointing I can make her understand me in that tongue and she tells me the Russian words which I immediately hunt up in my dictionary, to make sure of their spelling. Unfortunately there lives next to me, separated only by a thin door, a French officer, and he has taken to batting on the door every time he hears us "strafing" the hated language. If he realised how I was murdering the Kaiser's German, he'd recommend me for a St. Vladimir Cross at the very least.

After dinner tonight, old Mr. P—— of Boston dropped in to borrow some books. We chatted and our talk soon turned to Rasputin, a never-failing topic these days. He remarked with true New England disgust that Rasputin was the most immoral man in Russia; and a man of tremendous magnetic and physical powers. He has heard that the reason for the murder was not politics but involved an intimacy between the self-styled monk and the wife of one of the high persons implicated. At any rate, Rasputin was invited to 94 Moika, Prince Yussupoff's house, was met there by his host, with the Grand Duke Dmitri Pavlovich, Purishkevich, and others, and after some preliminaries was ordered to commit suicide. When he refused, one of them, reputedly Purishkevich, took the pistol and shot him. His body was taken across the Islands and dropped off one of the far bridges through a hole in the ice. The rope and weight slipped off, so that the corpse floated and was found.

Armour tells me that a few days afterwards he drove across the same bridge and that his driver pointed out the hole, crossed himself and said, "It has not frozen; he was a saint!"

Friday, January 26. A quiet day until 11 P.M. At that hour I went to Capt. M——'s where I found a gay supper party in progress. The guests included the American Ambassador and two of his staff, a Russian general and his wife, an American banker, his wife and daughter, a cavalry captain stunning in a deep-red Caucasian uniform, an American special correspondent and her husband, and a British torpedo expert. After supper we danced until 3:00 A.M.

Saturday, January 27. On my way to work this morning I passed the church of St. Panteleimon the Martyr just as they began to ring its chimes. I never heard better rag-time. The big bells boomed, while the little ones tinkled a syncopated anthem which showed a truly "Ragtime Temple Bells" spirit in the heart of the bell-ringer. After work, I walked along the Moika Canal almost to the Marinsky Theatre to see the house where Rasputin was killed. It is new, square and ugly.

I dined with our Embassy's Commercial Attaché. After dinner he and I went out to a reception at the apartment of Harold Williams, author of *Russia of the Russians*. Mrs. Williams is a very clever Russian woman and their apartment is a great rendezvous for liberals of all sorts. Mr. Williams has lived in this country for a dozen years and represents the *London Chronicle*.

There was a great crowd there, mostly speaking Russian. I talked with Mr. Williams, with Ransom of the London *Daily News*, and with Capt. Grenfell, the British Naval Attaché. I met Mr. Guchkoff, Mr. Shidlovsky, and several other Duma Members. At supper I was placed between Mr. Williams and a Mme. Protopopoff, who assured me hastily that she was no relation to the Home Minister. She spoke French and we talked about Tolstoi and things Russian, with the constant feeling on my part that she would prefer to listen to the animated Russian conversation going on around us. Huntington had a headache and left early; I departed about midnight, although the party was still in full swing. I understand that shortly afterwards Prof. Miliukoff arrived and the conversation became distinctly political.

Sunday, January 28. Graham Taylor dropped in from Moscow this morning. He could not get a room at any hotel, so I am having an extra bed wedged into my palatial suite.

There are said to be a million strangers, mostly refugees from Poland and Lithuania, in Petrograd at present. Every hotel is jammed and no house or apartment for rent stays on the market for twenty-four hours. Guests sleep in the private dining-rooms and the corridors of the hotels, and one can never get a bath before nine A.M. or after nine P.M. because some unfortunate is bedded down in every bathroom. I verified this yesterday, for when at eight in the morning I sceptically entered the near-by bathroom, clad in bathrobe, slippers and towel, I tripped over a poor wretch sleeping on a mattress on the floor.

This morning we went with one of the American secretaries to inspect the German Embassy. I have noticed the building before and consider it an insult to St. Isaac's Cathedral opposite. It is the worst type of new German taste, built of iron-grey stone with frowning square pillars from sidewalk to cornice. The interior must have been dreadful in its first glory,   gilt and black and "kaiserliche und königliche" aggressive. Now it is all most picturesquely wrecked, a complete wholehearted Russian job. Furniture and fixtures are torn to pieces, wall paper scarred, door-handles and panels broken, ink spattered everywhere. Portraits, tapestries and carpets are ripped and torn. As art critics the Russians are soul-satisfying. The great entrance-hall and the corridors are piled high with broken furniture and statuary. Even the bathtubs,   of which we could find only three in that great building,   are broken or bent. The massive iron equestrian figures on the roof were torn down and thrown into the Moika Canal, where they floated, as they were only tin. Their salvaged remains still lie in the courtyard. All this took place a few weeks after war was declared. It is said that police agents directed the mob.

We supped at Eugene Prince's on the Petersburg side. His sister, who is a Red Cross nurse and was recently married to Capt. Afanasieff of the Russian Army, entertained us with stories of the front and showed us her war photographs, many of which were extraordinary. Some of the best were of the Russian priests conducting services on the battle line. Mme. Afanasieff's stories and pictures showed people living a happy normal outdoor life in spite of trenches, aeroplane shelters and heavy ordnance. Only a picture or two of dead soldiers torn by shrapnel reminded us of the ghastly business in which these smiling cheery officers and nurses were engaged.

Tuesday, January 30. There are still plenty of Russian soldiers, judging from what one sees here. They are a husky, healthy lot, and from my views of the recruits I do not think the quality of the material is deteriorating. At drill they are like children. If a recruit is abnormally awkward, the rest of his squad will stop work entirely and roar with laughter at his efforts. A friend tells me that he saw a recruit squad with one particularly clumsy member; the officer, when he had corrected him a dozen times, lost patience and stepping silently leapt upon him, striking with both feet in the small of his back and knocking him onto his face. The recruit rose sheepishly and immediately began getting the idea better.

There are innumerable men of military age driving truck-sledges, cleaning the streets and doing all sorts of other work. It will take many years to exhaust Russia's man-power.

I don't gather that the armies lost many men in Roumania. The Russians have fought one of those punishing man-saving rear-guard campaigns at which they are so superior. They seem to loathe the Roumanians and tell all sorts of slurring stories about them. It is said that the complete wrecking of the Roumanian oil fields, done so well that Germany will not get a cupful of oil for several years, was borne with great stoicism in this country.

Chapter II
Rumblings

Wednesday, January 31. There is no doubt that a revolution is coming. G—— says that in the provinces it is regarded as certain, and that people think it will be very bloody.[1]

The Tsar's actions alone are enough to provoke a revolt. Last fall he put into office the pro-German Stürmer. The latter immediately attacked the Zemstvo Union as a detriment to the war, but his own Ministers of War and Marine, acting upon representations from Generals Alexeieff, Ruzsky, and Brusiloff, reported that they could not get along without the Union. This fiasco and Miliukoff's denunciation of Stürmer in the Duma, drove him from office, the first time popular opinion has been able to exert such strength. The Tsar is said to have asked the recall of Sir George Buchanan, the British Ambassador, as an accomplice of Miliukoff, but to have met with a prompt refusal from Great Britain. Then Trepoff went in as a liberal, but the Tsar saddled him with Protopopoff, the worst reactionary of all, as Home Minister controlling the police and the press. While the Premier was expostulating and Nikolas vacillating, Rasputin was killed and the Tsar immediately grew stubborn, confirmed Protopopoff and forced Trepoff out. Now we have a nice old reactionary philanthropist as nominal head of the ministry, with Protopopoff as the real government. The Duma has been adjourned and while it is scheduled to assemble on February 27th, the wise ones say it will never meet. Meanwhile the throne has fewer adherents every day.

Thursday, February 1. We have just heard the unbelievable news of Germany's submarine-zone proclamation. If the report is true, it shows that Germany is on her last legs. It surely means that we enter the war.

Friday, February 2. No official news. The papers give the boundaries of the submarine zone. Will the Scandinavian steamers sail with our precious mail?

Graham and I went after lunch to the Alexander III Museum to see the pictures by Russian artists. It is a fine collection, but I found the much-talked-of Vereshchagins rather a disappointment. The landscapes and a few of the Cossack pictures pleased me most. It is interesting to contrast these superb landscapes with the totally

---

[1] G—— is most likely A. I. Guchkov.

unreal paintings of the sea; the Russians don't seem to understand the latter element. We dined at Donan's, and I went home to work.

Saturday, February 3. When I came from work this afternoon and entered the Palace Square from the Millionaya, I saw a picture only equalled by the Champs-Élysées and the Arc de Triomphe on a May afternoon. The sun was setting behind the Admiralty Gardens, and the golden needle of the Admiralty Spire and the faultless dome of St. Isaac's stood out against a sky supremely rosy and beautiful. The square was darkening fast, and the Alexander Column, the grim old Winter Palace, and the crescent of stately government buildings with the chariot-topped Morskaya Arch to break their mass, were all toned down to a shadowy softness. I stood and stood, wishing I were Joshua to stop the sun and prolong the delight.

Sunday, February 4. Graham Taylor left this noon. His visit has been a great treat.

I went to the Embassy after lunch and found many people there making inquiries. Most of the newspaper men in town were on hand. I had some talk with the Belgian minister; also a long session with Shershevsky, a political editor of the *Novoye Vremya*, a nice little chap with a military uniform and a bad limp. Everyone is greatly excited, and all believe a break with Germany is inevitable, with war to follow. I spent an hour telling the Russian journalists what immense industrial resources and man power the United States could put into a war if she were roused. One of them asked if the Ford factory could make submarines and aeroplanes, and A who had joined us, offered the whole establishment as if it were his own.[2]

Monday, February 5. Still no definite news. The papers think we have broken relations with Germany.

Tuesday, February 6. I dined with H—— whom I like very much. He tells me that in his opinion the great bulk of Russian trade in retail merchants' supplies will be captured by Germany again after the war. Neither the United States nor England can compete with her in prompt deliveries, long credits, nor the exact meeting of the buyers' needs. In machinery, steel and iron products, railroad and electrical supplies and in financing Russian manufacturers, we can lead the world if we will put aside provincialism and go at it in a big way. I pointed out that in financing one has to look to the law for protection and that the Russian administration of the law is so lax and so corrupt that it frightens away capital. He thought this a very good point, and said that the business people were beginning to realise it and to turn against the present bureaucratic government which they, as conservatives, had tried to support before. Everyone is gradually coming to see that this unfair, inefficient government must go.

Wednesday, February 7. They clean the streets of this city well. It has been cold steadily since I arrived, usually well below zero Fahrenheit, and it snows often. If they did not clear the streets frequently, the spring thaw would be a disaster. There seem to be plenty of husky men to chop and cart snow.

Thursday, February 8. Petrograd is more uneven in appearance than any other city I have seen. The guide books call the Mokhovaya, the Sergievskaya and the Fourshtadskaya fashionable streets, but we have nothing in American cities that combines handsome residence buildings and cheap tawdry shops as do these streets. The Mokhovaya, in particular, is spotted with middle-class stores throughout its entire length.

The Fourshtadskaya has a couple of barracks, several cheap *traktirs* (tea-house saloons) and a coal yard. The pictured shop-signs, portraying with a fine disregard for proportions the various wares offered, be they beeves, boots, thimbles or asparagus, may assist the illiterate peasant to shop, but they do not help the artistic eye to enjoy the architectural effects of these so-called residence streets.

As I walked home along the quays tonight, the sun was setting right behind the Petropavlovsk Fortress, and the gold spire of the Peter and Paul Cathedral, outlined against it, was marvellously beautiful. The haze of the Petrograd marshes, which we dread twenty-three hours a day, redeems itself gloriously at sunset time.

Friday, February 9. We seem to have broken with Germany. We hear all sorts of stories about Ambassador Gerard, that he has gone to Copenhagen, that he is detained in Berlin till Bernstorff's safety is assured, that he has gone to Switzerland.

I dined at Donan's Restaurant with Whitehouse and two other diplomats. Most of the talk was of war and America's part in it.

I heard some interesting things about the frustrations met in trying to do business with the Russian bureaucracy. Nowadays the stand-patters of the General Staff are paramount and anything that they do not understand, which includes almost everything in God's world, they veto. Repatriation of certain types of prisoners, women, old men, etc., has been solemnly agreed to for over a year, and the Palmyra hotel here is full of Germans for whom the preliminary repatriation order has been given. McClelland of our Petrograd consulate is the temporary boniface. Yet for months not one soul has been allowed to depart from Petrograd for Germany. Recently an important German lady died in the hotel, and our Embassy told the Foreign Office that the latter was responsible for her death. The Foreign Office was disconsolate, as it had arranged to exchange this woman for an important Russian lady whom it wanted very much. It blamed the delay on an old brigadier of the General Staff who does not believe in repatriation.

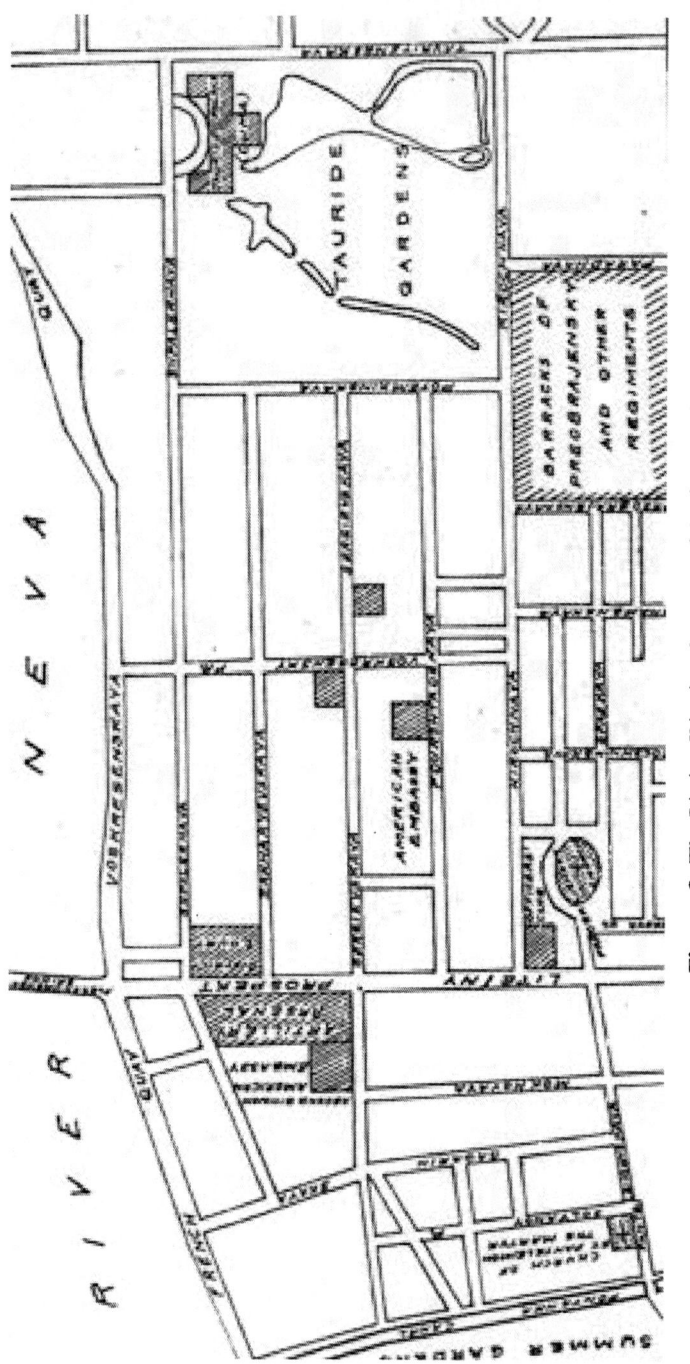

Figure 2. The Liteiny District, the scene of the first revolt.

Saturday, February 10. I am entertaining at dinner and the French Theatre next Tuesday. I went around this morning to get tickets, and when I passed the Resurrection Church, I dropped in for a minute or two. A gold-robed priest was celebrating morning prayer before a many-pictured altar, a sonorous male choir was chanting within, and in the nave a group of soldiers and common people were crossing themselves. The interior of the church is very gorgeous, lofty and picturesque, much more pleasing and uplifting than its bulbous exterior. I went specially to the spot where, under a marble canopy, one can still see the bloodstained street-paving on which Alexander II fell, mortally wounded. Poor vacillating Tsar, who went further toward reform than any of his ancestors had dared, but not far enough!

Afternoon   Bad news for my dinner-party! as it has just been decided that I go to Moscow tomorrow.

Sunday, February 11. I started at 10:30 P.M. with Philip Piatt for a five-day trip to Moscow.

Monday, February 12. This Nikolai Railroad is a traveller's joy; it has practically no curve nor grade from Petrograd to Moscow and is the easiest railroad in the world on which to sleep comfortably. And fares are ridiculously low. It costs R 21.75 (about $6.50 at present exchange) for first-class ticket and berth for the 400-mile trip and R 12.50, or $3.75, for a second-class ticket and berth.

We reached Moscow at one this afternoon. On our way from the station to the office the isvoshchik lost himself completely and took us far around the inner boulevards.[3] At the crest of the hill above the Hermitage Restaurant, we looked down on the river valley and half of the city, and marvelled at the innumerable gilded church-domes.

On our way from the office to the National Hotel we passed the walls and quaint old Vladimir Gate of the Chinese Town with its two churches, quite a fascinating picture in the winter twilight. At the hotel I stowed myself in Graham's room while Piatt was assigned to a private dining-room (for which they are charging him a la carte prices).

Mr. Varkala of the International Harvester Company, erstwhile of the University Settlement, Chicago, came to dinner and brought with him Mr. Narushevich, another Lithuanian, who is chief engineer of the Moscow City Railway. The latter talked little English, but we struggled along and finally got onto Lithuanian history, a subject I had just been plodding through in *The Mongols in Russia*. I talked of Gedimin and Olgerd and Vitold and Yagello as if they were members of my family and Mr. Narushevich was much excited and pleased. Finally after dilating on the greatness of his race, he asked, "How do people at large in America feel about the independence of Lithuania?" I hadn't the heart to tell him that most Americans thought Lithuania was a mineral water, so I "passed the buck" to Graham, who paused for a long breath and answered most diplomatically.

Mr. N. says there are only 3,000 tram cars in all Russia and that one-half of that number is in this city. There isn't an adequate street-car service in the entire empire. The municipality of Moscow is working on a plan for a cross-shaped subway, an improvement tremendously needed.

After dinner G. and I went to a vaudeville show at the "Letuchny Muish," a famous and characteristic Russian music hall. It was in a cellar, and the pit and the gallery were furnished with long tables. The performance was very amateurish but uproariously amusing, a series of one act plays, tableaux, songs or stunts, all done well and with careless buoyancy. Between the numbers, an announcer kept up a running fire of comments, being often answered by the audience and getting into arguments which caused great laughter.

Tuesday, February 13. At about three, Graham, Piatt and I quit work to go sightseeing. We started for the Kremlin but stopped at the Iberian Gate of the old city to see the holy shrine of the Virgin. The unobtrusive little building (not more than fifteen feet square) was crowded with worshippers, all busy buying and lighting candles, praying and crossing themselves, kissing the glass over the ikons with which every inch of wall is covered. Before the shrine, men and women knelt on the snow of the open square and prayed, the men uncovered in that icy weather. It was a wonderful and inspiring display of religious fervour, sincere and trustful and lacking any note of superstitious fear.

We passed through the Red Square into the Kremlin, and inspected the long rows of cannons captured from Napoleon's army and the two curiosities called "Tsar," the cannon that will not fire and the bell that will not ring. We tried to get into the churches but found that they had all closed at four o'clock. So we consoled ourselves with a general survey and departed through the Holy Gate. Then we explored that bulbous atrocity, the Church of Vassili Blajenni. Each of the eleven turrets covers a chapel, four in the basement and seven upstairs. Each is tiny, cramped and unimpressive. From the dome above each chapel there looks down the likeness of the person to whom it is dedicated, Father, Son, Holy Ghost, Virgin, or Saint, a most surprising effect for the visitor, to look up and find great eyes staring down upon him.

G. and I dined at the Praga Restaurant, where we ran into our intelligent Russian friend, who joined us at our table and told us many interesting things. The business community regards a revolution as inevitable and favors it, since present conditions are unbearable. The old order has practically no support outside of the court and bureaucracy. The people are all alienated except a few of the peasantry; the army (including many of the officers) is rank with republicanism; the merchant classes are disgusted; and most of the nobility are sick of graft and inefficiency and his business friends are all keen for a revolution, but doubt if it will come while the war lasts. They think that it will be very bloody and destructive.

He told us about Miliukoff's speech in the Duma which quoted the satisfaction of the German papers over Stürmer's appointment, a piece of oratory which was only possible because Rodzianko, the president of the Duma, had left the hall after calling to the chair one of the few deputies who did not understand the German language. The bureaucratic Eight objected noisily to Miliukoff's introduction of quotations in German, but the chairman said, "I can't understand a word he's saying, so why should I interfere?" Miliukoff is said to have taken refuge in the British Embassy when his life was threatened because of this speech. Stürmer fell, and the danger of a separate peace went with him. But the Tsar was furious and Trepoff never had a chance.

Graham and I went after dinner (at which we sat till 11 P.M.) to a tawdry cabaret theatre called Maxim's, run by an American negro, but were bored and didn't stay long.

Wednesday, February 14. S—— says that when he came to Moscow six months ago, he found his office full of German spies and a perfect channel for communication between war prisoners and the Fatherland; furthermore, that the Moscow police knew it and were opening every letter addressed there. He had a bitter fight to get rid of some of the spies. He finally routed them out, despite their wailing and gnashing of teeth, by the threat to let the police examine all records. The regular work was entirely neglected. To this day he occasionally finds in desk drawers hundreds of unanswered letters received a year ago.

Thursday, February 15. Piatt and I go to Petrograd at midnight tonight. To relieve freight congestion the Government has discontinued all passenger trains on main lines except one a day; and we've had a hectic time getting tickets and a compartment.

This is a church holiday, and G. and I went out to Lyubertsi, the Harvester Company's industrial town ten miles out, to ski with the Varkalas. Four of us started straight across country from the edge of the town, bound for the monastery of St. Nikolai Ugreshchi six miles away. The travelling was up-hill and downdale, but the snow was fairly hard and the air clear and exhilarating. We came to no fences nor boundary marks till we neared the monastery. The roads seemed to wander at haphazard across great open fields bounded only by hills and occasional clumps of trees or bushes. We passed a squatty village and on the hill above it a white gold-domed Russian church. After an hour we came out on the top of steep slopes above the valley of the Moskva River, and saw far below us the steeples and domes of the monastery. Here we had glorious coasting, so good that we climbed up and tried it again. On the second trip down, I carelessly raised one foot and had the pleasure of seeing my ski dash off down the hill ahead of me. Of course I had a beautiful fall and the rest of the slide was a mélange of hopping, tripping and bad language.

We devoured a picnic lunch in the hospice of the monastery. Afterwards we were shown over the queer old place, saw its three churches, and admired its jewel-covered sacred ikons, especially the miraculous picture of St. Nikolas, which four hundred years ago the Grand Prince Dmitri, fleeing in an hour of need, found hanging in a tree that grew on this very spot. Legend says that the Prince forthwith turned and wiped up the earth with his Tartar foes; and then founded this monastery.

We visited the enclosure of the monks who have foresworn the world and never go outside. We just missed an interview with the penitent Hermogen, ex-bishop of Saratoff, who is disciplined here for his direction of the activities of the eloquent fanatic Iliodor. It was under his influence that Iliodor gave up protecting the Tsar from the Duma and began protecting him from the bureaucracy.

After a frigid ride home and supper, we took a train back to Moscow. I rode with H—— one of the guests. He told me that the Russian War Department is completely paralysed and helpless, and that this curtailment of passenger traffic on the railroads is a measure of desperation. There are 25,000,000 poods[4] of freight piled up in Vladivostok. He believes that German trade will pick up right after the war and that much of it is going on through Sweden now. The Swedes have suddenly put consuls everywhere. Shortly after the war began, a lace firm in Kharkoff, which formerly bought from a German house, began figuring with an English concern; the latter wanted higher prices arid hard credit terms. One day the Kharkoff firm got a letter from their former suppliers in Germany saying, "We hear you are figuring with an English house. This is to notify you that you can still get our goods through So-and-so in Stockholm, at pre-war prices, and we will give you full credit until after the war." The English firm didn't get the order.

Labor conditions have improved immensely in Russia and wages have been multiplied by five. Woman's lot is infinitely happier, with high wages and the abolition of vodka. A decent government need fear nothing from the people, but this fiasco of a system is constantly in danger of a revolution.

Friday, February 16. Got to Petrograd about three. Our train had no dining-car, but there were frequent ten-minute stops for meals, and station-restaurant food is not bad. We saw no freight moving despite the fact that this is the third day of curtailed passenger service. We have been told that the rolling stock is in such shocking condition that it must all be overhauled before large freight movements are possible.

Dosch-Fleurot of the N.Y. World[5] and Piatt dined in my rooms. Dosch was in Belgium during the first year of the war until the Germans chased him out, and Piatt had just come from the Belief Commission; so we had a Belgian evening.

Saturday, February 17. The bread lines in Petrograd seem to have grown noticeably longer and slower in the week I have been away. I have seen bread lines on certain days ever since I reached Russia, but they did not seem irksome nor much of a hardship. In Moscow they were noisy, good-natured affairs, but tediously slow.

There is much talk of the distinctly pro-Duma attitude of the British Commission which is in Russia now. At the British Banquet they got for guest of honor, not Golitzin the premier, but Rodzianko the president of the Duma. In Moscow the principal ceremony was the conferring of a decoration on the liberal mayor, a great enemy of the bureaucracy. When Golitzin urged Lord Milner to stay awhile and see Russia, the latter replied, "Yes, I want to study the workings of your great institution, the Duma, which meets so soon," referring to the conjectured plan of the bureaucracy to postpone again the reopening of the Duma which is set for February 27th. The British want to strengthen the Duma and forestall a revolution.

Sunday, February 18. Went to the English Church. When I got back to the hotel, I found Huntington waiting hungrily in my rooms and we went off to his apartment for lunch. Later we called on the Harold Williamses and had a very merry time although I don't know what most of it was about, since they talked Russian. H. has very good ideas on trade development, and on sympathy and good understanding with the Russians. His remarkable command of the Russian language gives him an entrée which few Americans have.

Monday, February 19. I heard yesterday the story of the spiritualist seance engineered by Protopopoff for the Tsar. It was at Tsarskoe Selo. The Tsar, Tsarina, their two eldest daughters, the minister and his right-hand man gathered around the table. Suddenly Protopopoff grew rigid, with set eyes and tense arms outstretched; then after some minutes he pulled himself together and said, "There has just appeared to me the spirit of St. Gregory Rasputin; and he bids us continue to strengthen the Holy Autocracy." The Tsar sat staring and believed every word of it. I hear this story is current, with some variations, and is regarded as gospel truth, in many "well-informed circles."

Had a breathless time getting my Moscow train this evening. At 7:30, with letters unfinished, trunks half-packed, hotel-bill unsettled, I found that it left at 8:30 instead of 10:30. One has to be an official or a foreigner to get a railroad ticket, and a mind-reader to catch a train in this misguided country.

Tuesday, February 20. Reached Moscow at noon, still mad and feeling pretty rocky into the bargain. The journey did not improve my temper nor my health.

I must learn to carry my own bed-linen and a teapot. An aged *chinovnik* who shared my compartment saved me from a general collapse by giving me a glass of his tea this morning. May he live to be a Real State Councillor and a civilian general!

I did not see a single car of freight moving on the key-railroad of Russia today.

At the office I found that my proofs from the printer, due two days ago, had not yet arrived. The printer's aunt had died and he had felt obliged to take a three-day holiday. If the deceased had been his wife, he would doubtless have taken a fortnight, and that would have carried him into Lent, in which every other day is a church holiday. And yet they say the Russians are overworked and down-trodden!

I came up to the Hotel National for lunch with the idea of taking a half-holiday myself. There I met Eugene Prince and a Dr. H—— and they lunched with me. Dr. H. is an American surgeon who has been over here for two years in charge of a hospital at Gen. Brusiloff's field headquarters and has the rank of colonel in the Russian army. He says that the common soldiers are almost insensible to pain and can easily be operated on without an anaesthetic. They are brave but lacking in ingenuity; with 50,000 American soldiers to break a hole in the German front, cut wires, demolish trenches, and get the Russians started, he believes they could start in tomorrow and advance to Warsaw and beyond. The Germans are about tired out and their line is very thin. Only the lack of initiative of the soldiers and the timid do-nothing-and-you'll-make-no-mistakes policy of the Russian commanders enable the enemy to hold on with so few men.

Dr. H. has often seen dead German machine-gun-men chained to their guns. These are volunteers who get extra pay for their work, which is no more dangerous than any other branch of the service.

Brusiloff is a good deal of a man. He is constantly hampered by the Tsarina, whom he hates. H. prophesies that the general will someday order her to be taken out and shot. All the army believe she is sending news to the Germans; and certainly the latter have surprising advance information of everything the Russians do. Once Brusiloff planned an attack but made it five days before the date set, catching the Germans off their guard and winning a great victory. Officer prisoners admitted that the attack came considerably before they expected it and were indignant at Russian perfidy. The Tsarina, too, was furious with Brusiloff and gave him a tongue-lashing, but he said, "I am responsible to no one but the Tsar," and turned on his heel and stalked out.

Chapter III
The Lull

Wednesday, February 21. There are lots of Chinese, Mongols, Sarts,[1] and Tartars in Moscow. Today I saw two Chinese women with bound feet, stumping along with market baskets on their arms. Their dress was the regular Chinese costume, black blouses and loose straight trousers.

Randolph, Taylor and I were invited to a benefit performance at the house of Mme. Mariya M———, a rich and charming young member of a famous Moscow family. This lady takes innumerable dancing lessons and does very artistic pas-seules. We arrived late at her big house out by the Red Gates, and as we came up the ceremonial staircase we saw our hostess at the top. She was wearing a gorgeous Russian costume and a stunning peacock's tail of pearls framed her charming visage. She waved her hand at us and called out, "Oh, you've missed my Russian dance and I did so want you to see it." She made us the guests of honor, sat at supper with us along with her younger sister and a handsome young Countess Something-or-other; she joined us between her dances, smiled on us and told us that her second husband was to be an American. (Her first she divorced three years ago.) Her second dance was a dainty Columbine affair, and her third a very pretty and effective gypsy dance. The intervening numbers were uninteresting. The entertainment was organised by a neighboring high-school, Mme. M-lending her house and her services. The audience was mostly middle-class and civilian; but in one corner was a little group of maimed soldiers, cheerful despite crutches, slings and bandages, who had been invited in from that part of the great house which our generous hostess had loaned to the Zemstvo Union for a lazarette.

Thursday, February 22. Graham and I met on the street Likiardopolis, an editor of the *Utro Rossi* newspaper, who told us that his paper had just been fined because of an editorial commending Lord Milner for conferring a decoration on such a prominent liberal as the Mayor of Moscow.

Lunched with S———. Some of his wife's relatives are court ladies and he says the Tsarina is generally hated and that much of the court and even some of the Roma-

---

[1] Sarts were people from central Asia. See March 25, n. 1, p. 99.

noffs favor a revolution. Apparently it is almost unanimous. S-is pessimistic as to the result.

Saturday, February 24. This is a holiday because the Russian Lent begins Monday. I went out this morning to ski in Sokolniki Park with a party mainly American, of which Mrs. McGowan and her charming daughters were the moving spirits.

In the evening G. and I went to a dance at the big house beyond the Red Gates, and had a most amusing time. On arriving we found our hostess' younger sister in command, supported by her fat step-brother, a lieutenant at home for a few days on leave. In one corner of the elaborately furnished salon sat the two attractive Misses Smith surrounded by all the English-speaking men; in another corner a group of Russian-speaking damsels chatted with an awkward-looking officer and an equally awkward-looking civilian; several unattached men hovered about restlessly. No one had a notion what to do. The younger sister giggled charmingly; we admired the paintings, some of them the handiwork of our hostess, and talked desultorily. So an hour passed. Then our hostess came in from the Charity Bazaar, clad in a brilliant peasant costume; with her came two of her friends dressed as gypsy fortune-tellers dark-haired dashing creatures, a pretty blond girl, and a funny active youngster with a little yellow beard. Things immediately woke up. Dancing began, all waltzes of course. The Smith girls waltz very well, Mme. M. moderately well, the rest quite badly. I took a great liking to one of the gypsies, whose first name was Natasha, and went out to supper with her. She talked French charmingly but no English. Beyond me two elderly men in sack-suits sat on either side of the hostess, and across the table was a bearded uncle-like fat man with celluloid cuffs. (In the provinces celluloid linen is a sign of nobility.) We walked home at 2 A.M. with the enthusiastic little bearded chap. It was very cold and there were no cars running, nor any isvoshchiks to be had.

Sunday, February 25. Tea this afternoon at the S———s'. Mrs. S. proves to be a most delightful Russian woman, very highly connected. She and her sister showed us beautiful boyar costumes and jewellery, and promised to go shopping with us later when we were ready to buy mementos.

G. and I dined at the Praga and went to the Charity Bazaar at the Savoy Theatre. We found our hostess of last night presiding at a very tawdry booth, but herself quite a landmark in another great Russian headdress of pearls. She received us with warmth and annexed some of our money in an unscientific gamble called Krasnaya Karta. She asked us to take her to supper in a few minutes. As a preliminary we went over and had our horoscopes read by that round-faced gypsy, Miss Natasha; who told me a very good fortune, including the fact that the affairs of the heart were going well and that the greatest success in that line would attend a long voyage I should soon take. (Mind you, she doesn't know I'm planning to marry.) Then Mme. M. joined us and we went to the supper room. It was jammed and we couldn't get a table. She wandered around visiting and shaking hands with people, and finally settled down at the Governor General's table and forgot all about us. Her name is Russian for Frost,[2] and there is something in a name this time. G. and I executed a quiet "sneak" for home and bed.

Monday, February 26. We called at noon on Gregory Alexeieff, secretary of the General Committee of the Union of Zemstvos; I presented a letter of introduction from Samuel Harper of the University of Chicago and we had a most satisfactory interview with him. He advises me to read Vinogradoff's "Self-Government of Russia" and promised to send other pamphlets on the war-work of the Union. He will then introduce me to various members of his committee. I expressed particular interest in the financial and industrial end.

The Zemstvo Union has a great stone building six or eight stories high on the Pekrovka, a principal business street; every inch of it is occupied and it is a place to gladden the heart of an American. The atmosphere is absolutely different from that musty file-an-application-and-wait-three-weeks air which oppresses one in the huge ministry buildings in Petrograd. The overhead conveyors for "passing the buck" are entirely lacking. The Union is taking care of all the wounded, is feeding and clothing the armies, operating tanneries, shoe-shops and commissaries, working with and directing the Peasant Co-operative Societies; in short, it is doing three-fourths of the work of the moribund War Office. What is more, it is doing it efficiently and honestly.

The good work of the Union is a thorn in the side of the bureaucracy, as the comparison of results is too discreditable to the government. So the latter interferes on every pretext. A few months ago the Military Governor of Moscow forbade all public meetings of the Union and dissolved a convention of Zemstvo presidents which was discussing the care of the wounded, the boot-supply, and other treasonable subjects. This stupid interference has deprived the government of the support of the last "die-hards" among the landed gentry. It is on a par with the recent outrageous arrest of the labor members of the War Industry Committee[3] in Petrograd.

At Mikhailoff's fur store this evening, I talked with a Belgian who was in Moscow in 1905. He described to me the riots, barricades and miscellaneous murder of that exciting time. The government picked out its most unruly regiments of Cossacks to quell the disturbance, and they shot at everything in sight. A man standing next to my informant in a side street leaned out to look up the Tverskaya and exposed his head and one hand; his hand was drilled clean through with a bullet. Lucky it wasn't his head! The word "Cossack" originally meant bandit and these fellows live up to their name. I shouldn't be surprised if the revolution which is coming will begin with

---

[2] The Russian word for frost is *moroz*.

[3] Footnote in original: This Committee was formed by the business men of Russia, aided by the labor leaders, to organize the production and purchase of munitions.

a massacre of the Cossacks comparable only to that of the Janissaries, or to Peter the Great's slaughter of the Strelsi.

Tuesday, February 27. An uneventful day at the office. Lunched at the Polish restaurant. Russian lesson at 5:30. Dined at the Hermitage.

While I was at the American Consulate, two Austrian military prisoners came in; they had been left behind by their escort and wanted nothing so much as to rejoin their own squad on its way to the prison camp. They were pitiful little shrimps. The consulate messenger refused to convoy them out to military headquarters, saying he was afraid for his life at the latter place. After some telephoning, the consul gave them a letter of identification and sent them out without escort. I sincerely pity them if they wander off the straight path from the consulate to the headquarters.

Wednesday, February 28. I walked to the office this morning with Randolph. He told me of a rumour that the opening of the Duma was interfered with and that a general strike has been started in Petrograd.

Graham Taylor and Hamilton dined with me. We hear that the Duma opened with wild speeches; that armored motor-cars and platoons of Cossacks patrolled the Nevsky. This may be idle talk; everything is placid as a millpond here.

Thursday, March 1. No truth in the above. Everything is quiet at Petrograd.

I called at 2:30 on Mme. G——, a clever Russian woman who lives in a big house at the corner of one of the main squares. The G——s are a rich merchant family, and their house is full of modern Russian paintings, quite an interesting collection.

We talked for an hour about current topics. She says that the Duma leaders offer very little advantage over the present ministers because they are not practical enough to form a successful administration even if they were given the chance. She deplores the lack of practicality in the leaders of the liberal movement. I ascribed this to (1) the penalty, in loss of organising and of executive ability, that a country pays for being agricultural rather than industrial; (2) the unworldly and kaleidoscopic idealism of the Intelligentsia who are called upon to lead and who are mostly professional men of no business experience; and (3) the indifference of the great middle-class, which does not call the best available talent into its service and then by organised effort and continuous public opinion force the government to progress. She said, "The Intelligentsia mean well, but they cannot even govern their own lives; when they have a little money they live extravagantly, when they have none they live badly." No one wants a change to a feeble liberal government which would fail and cause reaction or a halting of the war.

She does not believe that there will be a revolution until after the war; and points to the patience of people in the bread lines as a reason for so thinking. There were strikes yesterday at some of the big factories here because the workmen were unable to get bread, but they were entirely peaceful and were easily settled. The people are almost too reasonable!

She believes that any revolution during the war would mean a separate peace, as there is said to be a clause in the alliance treaty which permits it in case of domestic insurrection. The government is using this clause as a club over the heads of would-be revolutionists. No one in Russia, except the desperately seared bureaucracy, wants a separate peace.

Of course the war might be continued in spite of a revolution if Grand Duke Nikolai Nikolaievich were called in from the Caucasus, but he is said to be drinking heavily and to be very sullen. Another possibility is Grand Duke Nikolai Mikhailovich, who is described as the most enlightened member of his tribe. He was the only man who dared applaud when Purishkevich made his famous attack on Rasputin in the Duma. Some leader who can overthrow the government and fight the war simultaneously is absolutely indispensable to a successful revolution.

Mme. G. does not believe a word of the stories of intimacy between Rasputin and the Tsarina. The latter she describes as very nervous and unhappy, always at high tension because of the hopeless ill-health of the Tsarevitch and the problem of succession; above all, a woman fearfully imperious with everybody; but for a long period of years very pro-English in sympathy, and entirely out of touch with her Hessian relations.

I asked about the friction between the Tzarina and Brusiloff. She said that my version of the encounter (see diary of Feb. 20) was quite distorted; she had the true story from Brusiloff's adjutant. The Tsarina is constantly interfering in matters pertaining to the conduct of the war, frequently going out to the front alone and confusing the General Staff with impossible orders. On the occasion in question the staff had issued an order for a simultaneous advance on all fronts on a given day. Brusiloff anticipated it by five days; conditions on his front were favorable earlier, he thought, and the results in ground gained and prisoners captured justified this conclusion. He reported to the Staff very much pleased with himself, and found the Tsarina there. She treated him to a tirade, which in a way was justified because the greatest problem has been to get the generals to work together. Brusiloff was naturally furious and retorted: "I am only responsible for my actions to His Majesty the Tsar." The Tsarina dismissed him angrily and later made the Tsar refuse to see him. The general was so despondent at this sign of ill-favor that his adjutant had to stay with him constantly to keep him from committing suicide.

Saturday, March 3. Until 2:30, 1 worked and wrote letters at the office without even stopping for lunch.

G. and I saw Prince off for Petrograd at 3:00 and then lunched at Filipoff's restaurant and bakery near the Post Office. At that hour there was still a long bread-line outside and only a small section counted out by a policeman was allowed to enter at one time. While we sat at lunch, a soldier in line inside the shop started a noisy argument with the cashier; suddenly from the restaurant part strode an officer and said one word; the soldier clapped his heels together and saluted, and we heard no more, not even a murmur, from him.

In a few moments the supply of bread gave out and about fifty persons, inside and out, were told they could get none. Such vociferous despair as was uttered by some women at the head of the line I never heard; those further back must have been desperate already for they slunk away without a word.

We supplemented our lunch with hot chocolate at Siou's tea shop on the Kuznetsky Most. There we met Griffin Barry, just in from Kazan, a pleasant chap in riding breeches, puttees and goloshes. I offered him a refuge for the night in my room as he couldn't get anything at any hotel. I was much interested in his description of the unhappy situation of a young English woman married to an elderly German who is interned in Kazan and is sick and cranky. The wife is of course free to travel but refuses to leave her husband, and no one in the town will have anything to do with her. One of the little tragedies of this war.

Sunday, March 4. Dined at the G——s', with a company of sixteen. At dinner I sat between the hostess and Mrs. Lockhart, wife of the British Consul, both of whom are charming. We talked mostly of the international situation, nothing original, and small talk. Someone said that in one of the bakeries the other day, at the time the bread gave out, the crowd spied three wagon-loads of flour in the back-yard. They seized them and found that they were consigned to the postmaster of Moscow and two other officials. People are beginning to rebel and to cry out that there is plenty for the rich and powerful, but only bread-cards and scarcity for the poor.

Russian manners are somewhat different from ours. Before entering the dining-room we stood around a table in the hall which was loaded with all sorts of hors d'œvres and liqueurs, and had a fair-sized meal of them. Throughout the dinner Mr. G. kept constantly rising and circulating about the table with a bottle in each hand, filling the glasses of his guests. I was the only man in full dress; the rest divided between dinner coats, frock-coats and cutaways. One man wore a black stock with a cutaway. A stout individual opposite me tucked his napkin into his collar at dinner.

Afterwards we had two tables of bridge and one of poker. I played bridge with Mme. Gr., Mrs. L., and a large Russian woman who had been late to dinner on account of hospital work. Very bad bridge it was, at 5 kopeks a point (true Russian recklessness!), and I came out 5 roubles behind. But the people were delightful, especially Mme. G.

Monday, March 5. Lunched heavily at the Polski Restaurant, with McGowan, Flack, Taylor and Barry. Flack has come from the Philippines and described travel in China and on the Trans-Siberian. We will probably all go home that way when war is declared on Germany.

Chocolate with Graham at Siou's to take the place of dinner. Then Hamilton dropped in at my room and at 8:00 we went down to the dining-room for a bite. We found the usual group of Embassy Delegates dining there. I had a long talk with Bakeman, who is a very real person, about his experiences with the Red Cross during the retreat from Serbia. The rest were discussing England's policy.

Bakeman tells me that at Pensa, the capital of his province, the police practise every evening with machine guns just outside the city; he has seen and heard them often. Getting ready for the revolution!

Wednesday, March 7. A busy day at the office. Among other events, we had a call from an ex-employé, a German woman who was dismissed as a spy. This woman used to have letters from German prisoners sent here, thinking that they would not be opened because of the American address. The Russians were clever enough to "catch on" and all our mail was censored indiscriminately. This time she came to get some letters which we were holding firmly and suspiciously and, foreseeing our refusal to part with them, she urged us to read them and give them to her if they were all right. S—— at first demurred, then agreed to take the matter under consideration, but told her that he would turn any suspicious letters over to the police. With that she went out like a lamb, and my guess is she will never come back.

Thursday, March 8. I dined with Fell; then I went out to call on the McGowans. They live just off the Povarskaya, which is full of handsome houses and is the street in which Tolstoi located the Rostoff house in *War and Peace*. It was a magnificent night, with a full moon in a clear sky over fluffy new snow. Walking home I passed along the Mokhovaya under the Kremlin battlements, and the moonlight effect on Ivan Veliki's tower and on the church domes and palaces was stunning. It's good to be alive on such a night, but one hates to be 7,000 miles from one's fiancée.

Friday, March 9. Russia is a great place in which not to do shopping. The salespeople simply don't want to wait on you, don't care whether you buy or not. The foreigners leave them far behind in trade and the best shops are manned with English, Belgians, Swedes and Baltickers. Formerly the Germans were the great shopkeepers of Russia.

This evening I went to the opera in the box of Maddin Summers, the American Consul, with Mr. and Mrs. Summers, the latter's sister, Bakeman, Pettit, Carnes and Lewis. It was at the Great Theatre, which is most impressive with its six tiers of thirty boxes each. The opera, Tchaikovsky's *Pikovaya Dama* ("Queen of Spades"), was very gay, with refreshing music, an exciting plot that travelled right along, and scenes which lent themselves to picturesque setting. It was very well done, though there were no famous singers in the cast.

Saturday, March 10. Explored the Kitaigorod (the Chinese Town, within the ancient walls that still surround a half-mile of city north of the Kremlin). Coming from the business district of the Lubyanka, I followed the parked boulevard along the north wall to the Varvarka Gate and then up past the house of the Boyars Romanoff. It stands on a side-hill above the courtyards of an old monastery, small, square, immaculately Russian, an exact type of the proudly simple Moscow of the days before Ivan the Terrible and the Time of Trouble. Somehow one cannot imagine the inhabitants of that house admiring the bulbous horrors of the Church of St. Vassili the Beatified, just beyond.

Then I entered the Kremlin through the Holy Gate, hat in hand, and went straight to the Uspenski, the Coronation Cathedral. I couldn't grasp its interior proportions because of a great scaffolding, but got an impression of very effective height. The walls are a veritable gallery of holy pictures, closely set in a golden framework, each showing only the faces and hands of its figures through openings in a sheer gold screen. Above, the walls are frescoed with heroic figures of saints, far up into the pillared vaults of the ceiling. The floor space is small, square and completely open except for pillars and the two garish pavilions containing the thrones of the Tsarina and of the Patriarch. In one corner a deep-voiced priest was rehearsing chants with two novices and making the scaffoldings vibrate with his thunderous tones. A voluble sexton pounced upon me, and proudly showed me his treasures, a nail from the True Cross, the tombs and relics of a half dozen early Russian saints and Patriarchs, and the "Vladimir" Virgin supposed to have been painted by St. Luke. This old painting is the best relic of all, since it undoubtedly came to Kief from Constantinople in the days of Vladimir Monomakh[4] and was carried in solemn procession from Kief to Vladimir, north of the Volga, when Monomakh's grandson, Prince Andrei Bogolyuboff (The Love of God), moved his capital northward before the increasing pressure of Jinghis Khan's titanic conquests.

It was snowing and blowing, but I couldn't resist the temptation of climbing Ivan Veliki's tower for its view of the city. Having safely reached earth from its precarious ice-coated heights, I walked through the palace yard to the middle gate and departed.

I had tea with the wife of the British Consul, and there met the wife and daughter of the French Consul. The talk was mostly of the terrible difficulties of keeping house. I judge that except for those who live in hotels, all are suffering alike from inability to get supplies. Prices are getting higher and the list of unobtainable necessities is longer every day. What will the end be?

---

[4] Vladimir II ruled as grand prince of Kievan Rus' from 1113 to 1125.

Dined at the H———s'. Was much interested in an account of the "pogrom" in Moscow in the first year of the war, when the mob suddenly rose up and began smashing everything German until the street-cars could not run on the Myasnitzky for the wreckage thrown from the windows.

Sunday, March 11. Fell and I went to the Cathedral of the Redeemer this morning for mass. It was most impressive. The great church was filled with people, all standing, with hardly a passage-way except the broad aisle from the altar-doors to the platform in the centre of the nave. And the crowd was entirely made up of working people; there was hardly a well-dressed person in the assemblage. We arrived in the middle of the service and inside the open gates of the great pictured Byzantine kiosk which serves as an altar, in the chancel, well beyond the transepts, we could see gold-robed priests preparing the communion. Presently the doors were closed and a heavy curtain slid over the broad open transom above. While some mystery was being performed within, we could see through the arabesques of the doors that candles were carried to and fro, two male choirs, placed in porches on either side of the kiosk, sang very beautifully. Then the wide center door swung open, two priests came from side gates each with a candelabrum, one with two candles and one with three, the saintly old archbishop came out of the altar, took the candelabra, made the sign of the cross with them and bowed, uttering a prayer. This was a sign for even more violent bowings and crossings on the part of the people than those to which we had become accustomed. Presently a procession of priests in gorgeous gold robes followed the archbishop down the broad lane to the platform in the very centre of the nave. I have never seen a sweeter face than that of this dear old man, his white beard streaming to his waist, his brow pressed with a mitre heavy with jewels and pictures. His voice was plaintive and sweet, too, as he read the prayers from a great gold book brought with much ceremony from the sanctuary and held by a kneeling priest during the reading. Two black-bearded priests sang the responses; one with a deep thunder-like voice which filled the high dome above and seemed to shake the four evangelists and the serried saints of the upper walls; the other, a weak-faced man with spectacles, with a bass voice clear as a clarion. The most impressive moment was a special prayer for the success of the war, when every soul in the great church knelt reverently. Then the procession marched back, soldiers pushing through the crowd and lining the way; the doors swung to and the service was over.

It was a marvellously clear day. We crossed the river and walked up and down the quay opposite the Kremlin; then went over to the Tretyakoff Museum. A line of people a block long were in the street in front of the entrance, awaiting a chance to see the pictures, and their progress was very slow; so we gave up and turned toward home. Everyone was in a holiday mood, smiling and courteous.

In the afternoon I called on Mme. G———, and found her without guests. I heard that the Municipal Union has been asked to tackle the food-supply problem, which is getting perfectly impossible; and has made its acceptance conditional on having control of the railroads, without which its officers feel it will only fail dismally. The Minister of Provisions said this week in the Duma that a few months ago he would not let himself believe what he heard about food conditions, but now he knows that the statements have under-described the actual situation. We hear there has been some rioting in Petrograd during the last day or so; a food store in the Kamenny Ostroff Prospekt broken into, the mob fired on, etc. Certainly all is quiet here, although distress is evident.

Chapter IV
The Revolt

Monday, March 12. Last night when I got on the train in Moscow, I found my reservation in a compartment with two men and a woman (or lady, I may fairly say). The train left at midnight; my ticket entitled me to one of the lowers and the lady sat in the other while a peasant of shop-keeper type dropped off to sleep in the upper above her. I removed collar, coat, and shoes, wrapped myself in my overcoat and prepared for sleep. Then the lady skilfully climbed a ladder and leaped into the other upper. Thus perfectly naturally and decorously we travelled together. Next morning we all conversed and a third man who proved to be a clerk for the Russian-American Chamber of Commerce produced some chewing-gum, which was an amusing novelty to the lady and the peasant.

At the Nikolaieff Station in Petrograd (where we arrived at 1:00 P.M.) the porter told me there were no *isvoshchiks*.[1] When I reached the front of the station, I knew instinctively that the revolution had begun. Not a vehicle in sight, except a stray truck-sledge or two, not a street-car on that usually busy square; only the people standing amazed on the sidewalks and a patrol of Cossacks riding placidly around the snow-covered road-way. A workman came and explained, and then showed me by gestures, that there had been shooting. Everything was so placid that it was hard to believe. I put on my extra overcoat under my fur coat, used the strap of the Moscow Consulate's mail pouch to couple up my big suitcase (a good 100-lb. load), swung them across my shoulder, grabbed my other suitcase, and started to foot it to the American Embassy a long mile away.

The broad roadways of the Nevsky were absolutely empty for two or three blocks, but beyond the Liteiny I thought I saw troops. In the side streets I traversed, knots of people were busily discussing the situation; everyone was excited and happy, and many laughed at my tottering steps.

My way took me right through the great barracks district of the Preobrajenskaya and everywhere I saw groups of soldiers in heated controversy; some of them were armed with guns and bayonets, some empty-handed. It was a sunny day, my two coats approximated a Turkish bath, and my pauses for rest grew longer and longer;

---

[1] *Izvozchik* = coachman.

during one of them, I found myself near an especially excited group of wranglers and soon was looking into the muzzles of the rifles which one faction was pointing at the other. To divert the storm, I went to the nearest of them and in stammering Russian asked my way to the American Embassy. They forgot their quarrel long enough to grin and tell me.

While I rested at the corner of the Kirochnaya, I watched officers trying vainly to make a battalion fall in; some of the soldiers refused, some gave their guns openly to street-boys, and walked away. A non-commissioned officer with a drawn revolver tried to assemble the men by chasing them and pointing his weapon at them, but many shrugged their shoulders and dodged him. A good part of the battalion, however, was assembling. The crowd on the opposite sidewalk told me that this was the Semenovsky Regiment of the Guards. Groups of mounted couriers, mostly bouncing infantrymen on sleigh horses, were dashing to and fro in the Voskresensky, apparently between this regiment and troops in the Sergievskaya. Envoy bearing automobiles, overloaded with soldiers and street-boys, did not hesitate to drive close to the forming ranks, where to the great joy of the crowd they bantered the loyalists and offered terms of surrender. The officers of the Semenovsky seemingly lacked the nerve to prevent the spreading mutiny.

Up to the time I reached the Embassy I did not hear a shot fired.

At that isle of safety I delivered the mail pouch and got permission to leave my baggage temporarily, as the one-and-a-half-mile walk to the hotel was more than I could face at that crisis.

I learned then and afterwards fragments of the story of the last few days. There had been numerous outbursts of fighting between the Cossacks, and the workmen and students. One of the Embassy staff had heard a student make an inflammatory speech on the Nevsky and had seen an officer shoot him dead, only to be himself killed by an indignant soldier. Huntington and Trissell had crossed the Nevsky right behind a firing-line of soldiers lying on the snow and shooting at random down the street. Policemen had fired into a crowd in the course of suppressing a bread demonstration over on the Petersburg side. All these are the old, old story of a workmen-and-student demonstration bloodily put down by the police and Cossacks.[2]

---

[2] Footnote in original: (After the revolution.) Many eyewitnesses tell me that the attacks on the people during the three days previous to the revolt of the troops had been carefully managed by the Cossacks so as to do as little harm as possible. The roughing was all good-natured and as gentle as was compatible with theatrical effect. The policemen showed their usual cold-blooded brutality, and it was noticed that wherever a Cossack could surreptitiously strike a policeman with his *nagaika* or saber, he did so gleefully. There is record of at least one policeman killed by an accidental (?) shot from a Cossack rifle. These wild warriors have always heretofore been kept isolated and encouraged to be barbarous. In this war the government has been obliged to use them in the trenches, and contact with other troops has taught them that unusual privileges are no fair exchange for human rights.

This morning, though, Turner of the Embassy passed the barracks of the Preobrajensky, Peter the Great's old bodyguard, and saw the entire regiment drawn up in hollow square and its colonel addressing it on the necessity of firing on the mob. Suddenly a soldier stepped from the ranks and, clubbing his rifle, struck down the speaker; and the greater part of the regiment seized and disarmed the other officers. A few blocks distant, in front of the Artillery Arsenal on the Liteiny, the soldiers of the Volynian Life-guards had shot the general in command, and practically the whole regiment had revolted. They were now preparing for a defence and were negotiating with other troops of the garrison to join them. This probably explains the errand of the excited horsemen I had recently seen on the Voskresensky.

After lunch I ran into Hamilton who reported that he had just come over from the Myedveyd Hotel and that he had seen street-fighting all through the intervening part of town. We both had business on the Sergievskaya near the Fontanka Canal and agreed to go together, but when we came to the Liteiny (the main street of the district) we were halted by riflery and machinegun fire. A real battle was in progress between the Volynians at the Sergievskaya and the loyal companies of the Semenovsky who had marched down the Kirochnaya and debouched onto the Liteiny two blocks further south. The insurgents had hastily thrown together a barricade of crates and boxes from the Arsenal, and for effect had wheeled out five field-guns, which apparently no one knew how to use. At one end of the barrier they had left a gap and through it were sending automobiles with attacking parties against the enemy, who lay or knelt in the open street to reply. These cars had riflemen lying on the fenders and crouching in the front seats and tonneaux, the chauffeurs (usually innocent neutrals) being the only ones very much exposed. We stood in the mouth of the Fourshtadskaya, half-way between the lines, and watched them catapult to our corner, discharge a broadside at the enemy and swing off past us into shelter, skidding beautifully on the hard snow. Crowds of citizens standing in the protection of the buildings shouted encouragement as they passed.

Presently we crossed by an alley into the Sergievskaya and had no trouble in getting to within ten yards of the end of the barricade. Here the crowds of spectators were especially thick and we could only catch glimpses of the gallant defenders at their work. At the curb beside us, soldiers were climbing into motors and taking position for their dash down the Liteiny. We could see no wounded but on the sidewalk

---

Thanks to the disaffection of the Cossacks, the rioting grew worse. On Saturday, the police tried to segregate the workmen, of the factories in the Viborg district and on the islands by guarding all the bridges. But the people swarmed across the ice and forced their way onto the Nevsky. Sunday was a day of rest; but the government knew that the lull would only intensify the turbulence of Monday. So they sent out the order to prepare the garrison for the declaration of martial law. It is said that many of the soldiers argued all Sunday night as to whether or not they would fire on the people.

were long trails of fresh blood. These led to a courtyard, but within we found only two very drunken soldiers.[3] For the most part the troops and the populace were quiet, smiling and cheerful, much more animated than the usual Petrograd street-crowd, but far from riotous. Shoppers would insist on walking along the sidewalks between the opposing forces, generally keeping close to the buildings as a concession to the occasion, but entering the stores and transacting business as usual. During lulls in the battle people scurried across the Liteiny just back of the barricade, between the firing squad and a line of crouching reserves. It looked so easy I suggested to Hamilton that we cross too, transact our business and then return for the final curtain about dark. He agreed, but other Americans with us talked so affectingly of bullet wounds and the "dear ones at home" that we gave up the plan.

Later we heard the details of the Liteiny battle told by those who had seen it from Armour's windows, six stories up and directly above the loyalist position. The Semenovsky contented themselves with firing and did not try to advance nor to make any flank attack. Consequently casualties were few. One revolutionist, either mad or drunk, climbed the barricade and with gun to shoulder walked straight up the street-car track toward the enemy, firing as he went. At a hundred paces he stopped, emptied his gun and stepped over into a doorway to reload. When he appeared again, a fusillade of shots sent him crumpling to the snow. Several spectators left niches of observation and unexcitedly dragged the body to shelter. Others presently showed the same indifference to fire, when a little boy who ran out too far to watch, had his leg broken by a stray bullet. No one bothered, though, to pick up the frisky little dog who played too near the Semenovsky and was shot. These casualties and a half-dozen in the two firing lines were all that the observers reported.

As darkness fell, the firing stopped as if by common consent and the Semenovsky marched back to their barracks. Within two minutes the Liteiny was swarming with people, before even the insurgents had time to call in their riflemen from "the trenches." Huntington and I joined the exultant throng at the Fourshtadskaya corner and with them passed through one of the gaps in the barricade into revolutionary territory. The District Court Building, which occupied a full block of frontage just beyond, was a roaring furnace of flames. As we stopped to gaze, the fire department arrived, and the brass-hatted captain halted uncertainly to ask the revolutionists what he would be allowed to do. Apparently his aid was rejected, for the fire-carts drew in to the opposite curb and the firemen perched idly on them, watching the flaming spectacle with open-mouthed admiration. A work-man told us that the building had contained a political prison and that the Military Governor of Petrograd had also had an office there.

---

[3] Footnote in original: This was the only drunkenness I saw during the Revolution. –J, L. H., Jr.

At the Second Division of the American Embassy, which adjoins the Artillery Arsenal, we learned that a captain and twenty loyal men of the Volynians had arrived by way of the back fence and were either guarding the Embassy or hiding, our friends could not tell which. The captain was telephoning frantically to know what he should do. The American official in charge thought that the building might be attacked, since it had once been the Austrian Embassy, and decided that it was unsafe for any of the female employés to continue to live there. I offered my room at the Hotel France as a refuge for four or five women, since I had arranged to live with Huntington in his apartment on the Voskresensky. It had become more riotous outside with the coming of darkness, and there was a steady fourth-of-July fusillade of shots; but we sent scouts down to the quays and they reported that all seemed quiet along the river.

Four of us men formed a convoy and we started for the hotel. As we reached the quay we heard great shouting and there jolted past us two big motor trucks loaded with soldiers and decorated with red flags. They stopped by the Suvoroff Monument for an argument and then turned across the Troitsky Bridge toward the Fortress of Peter and Paul and the turbulent Petersburg side.

We left the quays at the Hermitage and as we cross the Millionaya, saw the head of a column of troops coming out of the Palace Square. From the cheering crowd which accompanied them we knew that they were revolutionists, and McClelland and I waited on the sidewalk while they passed. They marched in perfect order singing the Marseillaise, and the sergeants and corporals who commanded them were equipped with the swords and in some cases with the field-glasses of officers. A civilian told us that this was the Pavlovsky Regiment of the Guard; which had wavered all day and was now joining the revolt. The crowd exulted over the new converts.

As we crossed the Palace Square, we saw another dark mass of troops come out of the main gate of the Winter Palace and turn toward the Millionaya. We were told that this was the Ismailovsky, another guard regiment, which had followed the example of the Pavlovsky, had disarmed its officers, killed a few of them, and then had held a dress-parade in the great court of the Winter Palace to show that it owned the town.

At the Hotel France, Whiffen of the Associated Press told me that the Duma had been adjourned till April by Imperial Order; but that it had refused to go home, had adopted a resolution declaring the present ministry overthrown and had demanded the appointment of another having the confidence of the people.

On our way home we caught up with the Pavlovsky and Ismailovsky, which had now taken possession of the Marsovo Pole. A sub-lieutenant in charge of a cordon on the Palace Quay courteously told us that all this part of the city was in the hands of "Nashi" ("Our men") and that we need fear nothing. We left Miles at the Second Division, stopped a minute to watch a crowd breaking into a bakery, passed again through the barricade where the soldiers were sitting around camp-fires, and then called at our Embassy to tell the Ambassador all we had seen and heard.

The Ambassador had heard that Rodzianko, president of the Duma, country gentleman of great wealth and brilliant orator, was to be the overshadowing figure of the revolution; that the office of the secret police had been sacked and all its records destroyed; and that all officers were being forcibly disarmed. He had been called up on the telephone by a lady who had been present at the death of an officer killed by soldiers for refusing to give up his sword.

When we got home to Huntington's apartment we found that the cook was feeding three soldiers in the kitchen. They were a fine trio of broad-chested youngsters, who said that they were strangers in Petrograd, southerners of the Volynian regiment which had been the first to revolt. The Semenovsky now have possession of their barracks so they think it wisest not to go home; furthermore the police are coming out of their hiding-places under cover of darkness and are shooting soldiers indiscriminately. But they are not worried for they know that the Semenovsky are determined to join the revolution to-morrow morning. We let them sleep in the kitchen, as a matter of course.

With the Duma, the entire Petrograd garrison and the people working together, this should be a real revolution.

Tuesday, March 13. The first thing I saw from the window this morning was a very angry soldier levelling his gun at someone just out of my range of vision, and fingering the trigger ominously. He was speaking rapidly and furiously. Fortunately he cooled off without firing. Next I saw two civilians dragging machine guns along the opposite sidewalk.

The revolutionists are guarding this building as if it were a treasury. Varia, the cook, says that several generals who are on the blacklist of the Revolution live here, especially a Gen. Stroukoff who owns a factory and treats his workmen very badly. He is supposed to be hiding in his apartment and the betting is that he will never get out alive.

Yesterday was the day of revolting troops. Every regiment of the garrison except one joined the revolt and this morning the Semenovsky have "come into camp and promised to be good Indians." Someone told me at the Embassy last night that he had seen two or three thousand Cossacks riding out quietly toward the southern suburbs, apparently without a single ounce of fight left in them. Petrograd is absolutely in the hands of the uprisen soldiers and workmen.

Today begins the long-needed house-cleaning and the police are the first refuse to be swept out. Many of them are resisting and meeting violent deaths. One shot a soldier on our corner this morning and was promptly bayoneted and beheaded, much to the horror of our little servant girl who chanced to be passing. They are tremendously hated, these police, for they are all husky fighting men who are needed at the front but instead stay at home and cruelly oppress the people. Now they seem to be bewildered; they hide in apartments and on roofs and take pot-shots at soldiers and have to be laboriously captured or killed outright.

Every police station in the city has been raided to-day and all the records thrown out of the windows and burned. I watched the wrecking of one almost next door to the American Embassy, and saw old identification books marked 1893 blazing away on the top of the pyre. If by some miracle the old order should be restored, the people at least will have the satisfaction of knowing that these masses of accumulated blackmail are gone forever.

In the various sackings of government stores, great quantities of goods and provisions were found which the government had claimed were entirely exhausted. This greatly exasperated the people. It is reported that the supply of many articles of food had been purposely curtailed by government officials for grafting purposes. Our cook has bought from soldiers at ridiculously low prices all sorts of supplies, bolts of cloth, flour, etc., etc., which were taken from government stores that had been refusing them to the people for months.

The first Socialist Manifesto is out; it urges the continuance of the war, the preservation of law and order among the people, of discipline among the troops, and the rapid forming of a provisional government.

When I crossed the Liteiny this morning on my way to work I saw soldiers shooting up the Panteleimonskaya toward the Preobrajensky Church. I went to within a few yards of them but could not find out who or where the enemy were. They seemed much in earnest, though, stepping forward a dozen at a time and firing all five shots before retiring to shelter.

At the Sergievskaya barricade I noted an automobile checker directing the movement of cars. The Revolutionists have commandeered all the motors in the city, have decked them with red flags and are using them for scouting and organisation purposes. These machines are often so loaded with soldiers that even the running boards are crowded and two outposts drape themselves on the front fenders. Limousine cars are peaceful enough in appearance at a distance, but as they approach one sees bayonets and rifle barrels protruding from the windows. There is a responsible man in each one of these cars, who reports at intervals to a designated checker.

I called at the Second Division of the Embassy and learned that its brave garrison of twenty refugees had departed. At about three last night someone from headquarters telephoned their captain to take them back to barracks, as all was forgiven and they would be supplied with a good meal and warm beds. They went, and have not returned.

A crowd passed the Embassy early this afternoon waving red banners and singing the Marseillaise. Eight in front of the building they captured an officer but he made a satisfactory explanation and they let him go. Two or three soldiers pointed guns at people watching them from the Embassy windows. Thanks to these fool police, the revolution objects to being watched from windows and it's unsafe to persist in the practice.

Not long after the aforementioned crowd passed, it was discovered that policemen were hidden in the sixth-story attic of an apartment building on the Sergievskaya just east of the Voskresensky and were firing out of two back windows at soldiers on the latter street and on the Fourshtadskaya. Sharpshooters began to reply from the corner near the Embassy; the crowd stood in a semicircle right behind them and watched, myself among them. People walked placidly along the sidewalks of both streets, the fire of the soldiery often going directly over their heads; once I saw the concussion knock a man's hat off. The wall around the two windows was whitewashed and show a puff of plaster whenever it was hit so we could keep track of the marksmanship. Occasionally a rifle-barrel would appear from the attic within and its recoil would show that the police were answering, but we could see no results. Once a motor-load of soldiers sped by and the men on the running-boards fired up in the general direction of the enemy, more picturesquely than effectively. Then of a sudden an arm with a sword was thrust out the window and waved in a circle. A soldier right beside me raised his rifle to aim at it, but was stopped by a cry of "'Nashi, nashi!" ("Ours!"); another further down the street did fire, but a comrade took a flying leap at him and sent him sprawling. Obviously the stronghold was captured. I went around to the front of the building and heard that five policemen had been found there, but after some waiting I abandoned hope of seeing them or their corpses and departed.

Then Platt, Turner and I went up to the Duma. The Shpalernaya was a wild concourse of disorganised troops and populace, all happy and good-natured. We could see that they were unloading great trucks of provisions into the main entrance of the Tauride Palace, as if the national assembly expected to be besieged. Presently we heard cheering and a squad of soldiers leading some prisoners turned into the driveway of the palace. This was the first indication we had had that any quarter was being given; the rumour was that all policemen were being exterminated ruthlessly. It seemed rather decent to give these hated enemies even a drumhead court-martial.

In our eagerness to see the reception of these prisoners at the Duma itself, we scrambled over the low iron fence into the garden and started climbing snowdrifts to reach the main portico. A sentinel hailed us and indicated, by the simple method of aiming his gun at us, that we were not wanted. All guns are loaded these days and they sometimes go off unexpectedly. So we did not stop to identify ourselves but withdrew to the street side of the fence.

Presently we saw a large group of prisoners led from a side entrance under heavy guard and I followed in the crowd and examined them carefully. There were a few policemen in their black uniforms, a scattering of real or pretended soldiers, a forkbearded old Father Abraham with a half-dozen other Jews, and a fair proportion of dvorniks (janitors) and doormen; but the great bulk were broad-shouldered thugs only to be identified as policemen out of uniform. Some were heavily bandaged and had to be dragged along. A few fidgeted nervously and hung back, but most were surprisingly stolid. Their escort was not numerically strong, and the first shout of the crowd sounded ominous. But not a hand was raised against them; the crowd jeered quite good-humouredly. Soon they turned off the Shpalernaya through a high wooden gate beside a warehouse, where soldiers stopped the crowd. I waited outside a few minutes expecting, yet dreading, to hear volley-fire. The death of the policeman on our corner this morning and the customary penalty of sniping seemed to justify the expectation. But I now believe they were taken to some extemporised prison.

Other crowds of prisoners were led by, but for the most part were turned back from the Duma by mounted Cossacks and directed straight into the aforementioned gate. Presently we heard cheering and through a path opened in the crowd there came at a dog-trot four diminutive students, each towering about four-feet-six in stature and carrying a rifle at least five-feet-six, surrounding a great hulk of a soldier whose height seemed about six-feet-six,--the most joyous guard and the most humiliated and cowed prisoner that we saw.

The roadway was a kaleidoscope of soldiers, armed and unarmed, civilians, mounted Cossacks, automobiles full of red-cross nurses and of uniformed students, and trucks packed tight with humanity and bristling with bayonets and red flags. At the corner of the Potemkinskaya we were passed by a speeding motor from which a student threw hand-bills; but we were not quick enough to get one although we scrambled for them manfully with soldiers and workmen.

At the Embassy corner we saw flashes of rifle-fire in at least two directions, and one shot passed so near us that we heard it whistle. It was growing dark and we could not make out who were skirmishing, but the thought surged in upon us that we might be taken for policemen. We were near home and by unanimous consent adjourned for the day. The streets of this city are no place for an innocent bystander tonight.

Chapter V
The News Bulletins of the Revolution

After two days without newspapers, Petrograd once more had a news service on Tuesday evening. It took the form of an official bulletin, some copies of which were pasted up in prominent places throughout the city, while others were thrown to the crowd from automobiles. This bulletin was edited and signed by a so-called Committee of Petrograd Journalists and was printed in the shops of the *Novoye Vremya*, the *Bourse Gazette*, the *Russkaya Volya*, and other newspapers. It took up about two-thirds of a single newspaper sheet of stock size. At the top was a title in scare-head type "Izvyestia" (News), followed by the statement in heavy type, "The newspapers will not appear. Events are occurring too rapidly. The people have a right to know what is happening."

The last sentence alone was a new charter of liberty for Russia. The items of the first bulletin, which I insert here in their entirety, are in themselves a short history of the Revolution:

Dissolution of the Imperial Duma

On the basis of Chapter Ninety-Nine of the Fundamental Imperial Law it is commanded:

The sitting of the Imperial Duma and Imperial Council is adjourned the 26th of February (Sunday, March 11[1]) of this year and the date of its reconvening is designated for not later than April, 1917, in dependence upon extraordinary circumstances.

The Directing Senate will not stop in the fulfillment of the necessary arrangements.

Under the actual signature of the own hand of his imperial majesty

Nikolas.
February 27 (March 12), 1917

---

[1] Footnote in original: All dates used in the bulletin are Old Style, thirteen days behind New Style. For the sake of clearness, I have inserted in parentheses the dates according to our own calendar.

At the Tsar's Headquarters, February 25 (March 10).
Countersigned: President of the Council of Ministers, Prince Nikolas Golitzyn.

Decision of the Imperial Duma

The elder council,[2] assembled in extraordinary session and informed of the ukase and dissolution, has ordained:

The Imperial Duma will not separate. All deputies will remain in their places.

Uprising of the Troops

On February 27 (Monday, March 12), there passed over to the revolutionary people the following military units: Volynian, Preobrajensky, Litovsky, Keksholmsky, and Sapper regiments.

On the side of the revolutionary people are nearly 25,000 from the military ranks.

Delegation of Revolutionary Troops at the Duma

About 1 P.M. a delegation from 25,000 revolting soldiers appeared at the Imperial Duma to inquire about the position occupied by the representatives of the people.

M. V. Rodzianko transmitted to the delegation the following unanimously-adopted resolution of the elder council:

"The basic watchword of the moment shines out as the abolition of the old authority and the substitution for it of the new. In the act of recognising this, the Imperial Duma will take a lively part, but for this before all else, order and quiet are indispensable."

At the same time the president of the Imperial Duma delivered to the delegates the texts of telegrams despatched to the Tsar at Headquarters, to chief of staff General Alexeieff and to the three generals in chief command at the front.

---

[2] Footnote in original: Committee of party leaders.

First Telegram of M. V. Rodzianko to the Tsar

On February 26 (Sunday, March 11), the president of the Imperial Duma despatched to the headquarters of the Tsar a telegram of the following tenor:

"The situation is serious. In the capital is anarchy. The government is paralysed. Transportation, the supply of provisions and fuel have come to complete disorder. Dissatisfaction is growing general. On the streets is occurring disorderly shooting. This is partly troops shooting one another. It is indispensable to entrust to a person having the confidence of the country the formation of a new ministry. It is impossible to hesitate. Every delay is equally fatal. I pray God that at this hour the responsibility does not fall on the Crowned Head."

Telegrams of M. V. Rodzianko to the Chief Commanders at the Fronts

On the same day, February 26, the president of the Imperial Duma quoted by telegraph to the commanders of all fronts the above-mentioned telegram, adding a request that they personally justify to the Tsar the changed attitude of the president of the Imperial Duma.

Answering Telegrams of Brusiloff and Ruzsky

General Brusiloff answered: "Your telegram received. I have done my duty before the country and the Tsar."

The telegram of General Ruzsky reads: "I have fulfilled my commission."

Second Telegram of the President of Imperial Duma to the Tsar

On February 27 (Monday, March 12), in the morning the President of the Imperial Duma addressed the Tsar in a second telegram of the following context:

"The situation is becoming worse. It is necessary to take measures quickly, for tomorrow will be too late. The final hour has come, when the fate of the country and the dynasty will be decided."

The Revolutionary Army at the Imperial Duma

About 2 P.M. a strong detachment of the revolutionary army, escorted by the armed populace, approached the building of the Imperial Duma. There went out to welcome the revolutionary army members of the Imperial Duma, N. S. Chkheidze, A. F. Kerensky, A. I. Skobeleff and many others. The appearance of the deputies and above all of those especially popular with the masses, was welcomed with noisy "hurrahs." Chkheidze, Kerensky and Skobeleff stepped forward and addressed the troops. The people, having conducted the revolted soldiers, relieved the sentinels at the Tauride Palace, assembled for themselves the guard over the Imperial Duma, took possession of the post and telegraph office at the Duma building and took over the time and telephone apparatus.

Session of the Imperial Duma

At 2:30 P.M. in the Duma Hall, under the presidency of M. V. Rodzianko, was held a conference of members of the Imperial Duma. In the deliberation was brought up the question of the organization of a temporary committee for keeping order in Petrograd and for intercourse with different institutions and persons. In the opinion of the numerous assembly, the choice of a temporary committee should be entrusted to the elder council to work out.

At the end of the meeting of the Imperial Duma there was held in the office of M. V. Rodzianko a session of the elder council at which took place an election of members for this Temporary Committee.

Committee of the Imperial Duma for the Establishment of Order in Petrograd and for Intercourse with Institutions and Persons in the Composition of the Temporary Committee were:

M. V. Rodzianko
N. V. Nekrasoff
A. I. Konovaloff

I. I. Dmitriukoff
A. F. Kerensky
N. S. Chkheidze
V. V. Shulgin
S. I. Shidlovsky
P. N. Miliukoff
M. A. Karauloff
V. N. Lvoff
V. A. Rjevsky

* * *

Arrest of the President of the Council of the Empire

About 5:30 P.M. (Monday, March 12) there was brought to the Imperial Duma, under a strong convoy of the revolutionary populace, the president of the Council of the Empire, former Minister of Justice I. G. Shcheglovitoff.

After a short conference, by arrangement of members of the Temporary Committee, Shcheglovitoff was temporarily placed under a strong guard in the Ministerial Pavilion of the Tauride Palace.

* * *

Capture of the Arsenal and Chief Artillary Headquarters

This morning the arsenal and chief artillery office were captured after a short struggle by the troops gone over to the revolutionary populace. They killed General Matusoff in command of the artillery warehouse. The arsenal and offices were put under a guard of revolutionists.

* * *

Capture of the "Crosses" and Liberation of the Politicals

Today the Viborg solitary-confinement prison "The Crosses" was captured by a strong force of soldiers and revolutionary populace after a short struggle. All political prisoners were released; among the number liberated were the labor group of the War Industry Committee; and also Khrustaleff-Nosar.

They also captured the house of preliminary confinement and the women's prison (Litovsky stronghold).

The Fall of the Fortress of Peter and Paul

Into the hands of the rebellious troops and the revolutionary populace fell also the Fortress of Peter and Paul, which was transformed into the head base of the revolutionary army. All political prisoners were released from the casemates and set at liberty.

Destruction of the Security Division

The Security Division[3] was destroyed and burned down. All archives and political matters were destroyed.

Resignation of Premier Golitzin

About 1 P.M. the President of the Council of Ministers called by telephone Duma President Rodzianko and offered him his resignation. According to rumor he gave also the resignations of the other members of the Cabinet, with the exception of Protopopoff.

During the day the revolutionists searched the houses of the old members of the cabinet. They could not arrest the ministers because none of the latter were found at home.

Council of Workmen's Deputies

During the day, there assembled in the premises of the Duma the representatives of the workmen, soldiers, and some of the socialist societies. They organised a Council of Workmen's Deputies, and decided to address an appeal to the populace.

---

[3] Footnote in original: The Secret Police.

The Appeal of the Workmen's Deputies

The Council of Workmen's Deputies ordered that an appeal should be addressed to the populace as follows:

Citizens, the representatives of the laborers and the soldiers and of the population of Petrograd, assembled in the Duma, declare that the first meeting of their representatives will be held today at 7:00 P.M., in the premises of the Duma. All the military units which have come to the side of the people are to choose one representative from each company. The factories are to elect their deputies, one for each thousand of laborers. Such factories as have less than one thousand laborers may elect one deputy each.

From the Temporary Committee of the Council of Workmen's Deputies

Citizens, the soldiers who took the part of the people have been in the streets since morning and are very hungry. The Council of Workmen's Deputies and of the Population are trying their best to feed the soldiers; but to organise the food supply is not so easy. Therefore the Council appeals to you citizens with the request to feed the soldiers with all that you can give them.

(Signed) Temporary Executive Committee of the Council of Workmen's Deputies, 27th of February, 1917.

The following items, together with long verbatim reports of the eloquent appeals of Rodzianko, Miliukoff and Kerensky to the various delegations visiting the Duma, make up the News Bulletin for Tuesday, March 13:

Problems of the Executive Committee of the Duma

The Temporary Committee of the Duma has defined its problems in the following way: The Duma aims to establish a bond between officers and the lower ranks. It feels the urgent necessity of organising the military masses; the progress has been better than was expected, but there is still no organisation. Events are happening too rapidly.

Therefore officers are invited to show all possible cooperation with the Imperial Duma in its heavy labor.

Order has so far been maintained by patrols appointed by the Military Committee of the Duma and by armed men in automobiles.

All possible steps are being taken to protect the Arsenal and the mint in the Peter-Paul Fortress. Hostile acts against the fortress are undesirable. All political prisoners who have hitherto languished in the casemates, and nineteen soldiers who were arrested in the last few days, have been liberated.

Notwithstanding profound differences of political and social ideals, the members of the Duma, having accomplished the formation of a Temporary Committee at the present difficult moment, have reached complete harmony among themselves. Before them and others stands the pressing task of organising an elemental popular movement.

The danger of disorganisation is likewise understood by all.

The slogan of the moment is "Citizens, organise. In organisation is salvation and strength. Obey the Temporary Committee of the Duma."

The Revolutionary Army

The number of revolting military units is growing from hour to hour. We can say with certainty that nearly the whole Petrograd garrison, with a few exceptions, is now on the side of the revolutionists. Some regiments joined the revolutionary camp in their entirety, led by their officers, among this number the Preobrajensky regiment.

Yesterday there were only a few officers on the side of the Revolution; today there are many of them, now ensigns, now sub-lieutenants, lieutenants, captains, and even generals.

The whole organisation of the new army is in the hands of the commander of the Petrograd garrison, Colonel of the General Staff and Member of the Duma, B. A. Engelhardt.

Every minute new military units arrive at the Tauride Palace. Some regiments come with flying flags and music, headed by their commanders.

In the Ekaterinsky hall of the palace the different military units are formed into battalions. They receive ammunition, and are sent to different parts of town, in conformation with an established plan.

All the orders are given in writing in the name of the commander of the Petrograd garrison, Colonel Engelhardt.

The Arrested

The Ministerial Pavilion of the Tauride Palace is filled to overflowing with prisoners of high ranks.

Besides I. G. Shcheglovitoff, who was arrested on the 27th of February (March 12), the following were brought in under guard at different periods of the day:

Former President of the Council of the Ministers B. V. Stürmer;
Former Assistant to the Minister of Internal Affairs Protopopoff;
Lieutenant-General P. G. Kurloff;
Ex-Minister of Public Health G. E. Rein;
Member of the Council of the Empire Shirinsky Shaklmiatoff;
The very well-known general, M. C. Komisaroff;
Assistant Minister of Ways of Communication I. P. Borisoff;
Chief of the Railway Department S. B. Bogasheff;
Head of the General Office of Military Schools, General Zabelin;
Chief of Police of Petrograd, Major-General Balk;
Chief of the Military Medical Academy, General Makavaeff;
Vice-Admiral Kartseff;
Admiral Girse;
and a number of lesser employees of the administration and police.

Latest News

The entire chancery of the Preobrajensky regiment, with all their archives, was brought over to the Duma.

The fourth Strelkovi, his Majesty's regiment, which is stationed at Tsarskoe Selo, has come over to the side of the people, and at 4 o'clock marched to the Tauride Palace.

At the Finland Railway Station there arrived three packets addressed to the Minister of Foreign Affairs. These packets were delivered to the Duma and turned over to P. N. Miliukoff.

The military units ordered by the old government from Strelna came over to the side of the revolution and proceeded to the Duma.

A revolutionary regiment has taken possession of the Ministry of Ways of Communication.

At three o'clock there arrived at the Duma a lieutenant-colonel of the General Staff, bringing a packet from the Chief of the General Staff addressed to the President of the Executive Committee of the Duma, M. V. Rodzianko.

V. A. Maklakoff has taken possession of the Circuit Court with a special patrol. On his motion the Court will continue its functions beginning tomorrow morning.

At four o'clock P.M. there arrived at the Duma the entire student body of the Military Medical Academy. At the Military Medical Academy itself a conference of professors is now being held to debate the events which are happening.

At two o'clock P.M. a member of the Duma, the priest Popoff II, blessed the Revolutionary Army, with a crucifix in his hands.

"God grant," said the clergyman, "that this day be memorable forever and ever."

Siberian Regiments

This morning two Siberian regiments arrived at the Nikolaieff Railway Station. Delegates from these regiments presented themselves at 11 o'clock at the Tauride and offered their services to the Temporary Committee of the Duma. Their offer was accepted with enthusiasm.

Tranquility of the Railway Lines

The Executive Committee of the Duma has received an official statement that the railway between Moscow and Petrograd is running normally.

Opening of the Banks

A conference of directors of banks and private credit institutions has decided, in view of the tranquillity of the population, to open all the banks.

Organisation of the City Militia

The temporary Executive Committee of the Duma ordered that Mr. M. A. Krizanovski, member of the City Duma, organise the Militia. For this purpose there was opened on the 28th day of February at 8 o'clock P.M. in the premises of the City Hall, an enrollment list for students of all the High Schools of Petrograd who would like to join the City Militia. The students were asked to appear with their High School certificates or other documents, to prove by identification that they have attended a High School.

The following are the leading articles of the morning and evening *Izvyestia* of Wednesday, March 14:

About 4 P.M. February 28th the Admiralty, where the members of the old government had been concealed, was occupied by the national troops.

Up to 12 o'clock there were three companies of the Izmailovsky Regiment and some mounted artillery and cavalry in the Admiralty. After twelve these troops, who had been on the side of the old regime, left the building and went home. After this the Ministers who had been in hiding there fled from the Admiralty.

At 11:15 P.M. a gentleman in a fur coat came to the Tauride Palace and asked a student there: "Tell me, you are a student?" "I am," said the student. "I would ask you please to take me to the members of the Executive Committee. I am the former Minister of the Interior, Protopopoff and I have always desired the welfare of our country and have therefore come voluntarily. Take me to whomever it is necessary."

The student took Mr. Protopopoff to the office of the Committee. The crowd and soldiers, recognising him, gave vent to exclamations of indignation. Pale and tottering, the ex-minister stood before one of the members. The latter, recognising him, sent for a convoy. The soldiers led him to the Ministerial Pavilion accompanied by an enormous procession. A. F. Kerensky, the Labor Leader, then appeared. The prisoner rose and going to him said: "Your Excellency, I place myself at your disposal." "Former Minister of the Interior Protopopoff," was the answer, "in the name of the Executive Committee I declare you arrested."

Protopopoff bowed to Kerensky and began to whisper something. On learning that the ex-Minister wanted to make some secret communication to him, Kerensky had a talk with him in a separate room, the contents of which will be given in this paper.

* * *

Further arrests made are as follows:
   Ex-Minister of Justice Dobrovolsky;
   Ex-Minister of Ways of Communication Kriger-Voinovsky;
   Former Director of Police Department and Ex-Chief of Police of Moscow, Gen. Klimovich;
   Assistant Chief of Petrograd Police, Lieut. Gen. Vendoff;
   Assistant Chief of Petrograd Police Lysogorsky, and all the chief members of the Prefecture;
   Dr. Dubrovin, President of the Union of Russian People.

The Committee announces that no arrests have been made by its orders, and in future arrests will be made only under special orders from the Committee. This declaration is made because there may be found to be among those arrested, persons whose arrest is not at all necessary.

In Moscow and Kharkoff the authority of the Temporary Committee of the National Duma has been recognised.

At 1:15 P.M. on Wednesday the Grand Duke Cyril Vladimirovich arrived at the Tauride Pallace. The Grand Duke was accompanied by the admiral commanding the Guard Equipage (Marines) and an escort of members of the Equipage.

The Grand Duke entered the Catherine Hall, and the President of the Duma M. V. Rodzianko was called out. Addressing him, the Grand Duke said:

"I have the honour to present myself to Your High Excellency. I am at your disposal. Like the whole nation I wish the welfare of Russia. This morning I explained to all the soldiers of the Guard Equipage the meaning of the events which were taking place and I can now declare that the whole Guard Equipage of the Fleet is at the complete disposal of the National Duma."

The words of the Grand Duke were met with cries of "Hurrah!"

M. V. Rodzianko thanked him and turning to the soldiers surrounding him, said: "I am very glad, men, to hear of the words of the Grand Duke. I felt sure that the Guard Equipage, as all the other troops, would fulfil their duty and help to cope with the common enemy and lead Russia to victory."

The words of the President of the Duma were also met with cheers.

Rodzianko then turning to the Grand Duke asked if he wished to remain in the Duma. The latter replied that the whole of the Guard Equipage was on its way to the Duma and that he wished to present them to its President.

"Then," said Rodzianko, "when you need me call me out." After this he returned to his office.

In view of the fact that all the quarters of the Duma are occupied, the representatives of the Committee of Petrograd Journalists proposed that the Grand Duke use their room. So the Admiral and the Adjutant of the Grand Duke accompanied him to the journalists' room.

The personal Convoy of His Majesty also presented themselves at the Duma and were met by M. A. Karauloff, representing the Executive Committee, who made a speech of welcome to them. Explaining the general position of things Karauloff called upon the Convoy to join the people in the defence of their interests.

This was met by loud hurrahs.

At the suggestion of Karauloff the Convoy immediately went to the barracks to arrest their officers who continued true to the old authority.

The officers of the Petrograd garrison who were in sympathy with the people, met in the Assembly Hall of the Army and Navy, at the suggestion of the Executive Committee. Fully realising that for the victorious ending of the war it was necessary to organise as swiftly as possible and to work behind the lines, they unanimously resolved:

To recognise the authority of the Executive Committee of the National Duma until the formation of a permanent Government.

Two members of the Duma, representatives of the Province of the Don Cossacks, visited the barracks of the First and Fourth Don Cossack regiments. The men were drawn up and the deputies made warm speeches praising their faithful service of the country and calling upon them to serve as faithfully the new government which was taking upon itself the defence of the fatherland.

The speech was met with cries of "Hurrah."

On Wednesday the Commandant of the Palace at Tsarskoe Selo telephoned to the President of the Executive Committee and requested that measures be taken to restore order in that suburb and especially in the district of the Palace.

At the order of the Executive Committee two members of the Duma were sent thither. All detachments of the Tsarskoe garrison have been ordered by the Executive Committee to remain in their places and maintain order.

Orders have been issued to the troops and militia of Petrograd as follows:

"There are immediately to be arrested all intoxicated persons, robbers, incendiaries, those firing in the air and, in general, disturbers of peace and order; those resisting persons who have special powers of any kind from the Executive Committee and persons serving in the protection of the city; all members of the police, of the secret police and of the Gendarme Corps; all persons who make searches in private apartments, or arrest private persons, especially members of the army, without being authorised to do so by the government.

All arrested persons are to be taken to various places of detention indicated, with the exception of high officials and generals, who, in case it is necessary to detain them, shall be taken to the Tauride Palace."

Signed, Member of the Temporary Committee, M. Karauloff.

An order has been issued that soldiers shall not deprive officers of their arms. The order to do so was never issued by the Committee.

The Petrograd Telegraph Agency has been taken over by the Committee and placed in charge of A. M. Lovyagin.

S. A. Adrianoff has been appointed Director.

Circular telegrams were immediately drawn up explaining all the events of the past three days and despatched "urgent" to all provincial newspapers.

To large cities like Kharkoff, Odessa, Kief, Saratoff and others supplementary telegrams have been sent explaining everything in great detail.

Practically all the employees remain.

The bulletins will in future be only for the provincial papers. They will be signed by P. P. Grensky.

The Winter Palace was occupied by revolutionary troops on Wednesday.

The central bureau of the city militia will be in the City Hall. Committees have been formed for each district. Each militiaman will be armed.

The supplies of flour in Petrograd are increasing, owing to the arrival of trains. Flour is being distributed by special automobiles to the bakeries for immediate baking.

Bulletins like these were published on every day of Revolution Week and were only discontinued on Sunday, March 18, when the regular Petrograd newspapers resumed publication.

Chapter VI
The New Order Replaces the Old

Wednesday, March 14. Last night our little servant-maid almost gave up the ghost. She had accumulated a hard cold from running around the streets for news, she and Varia the cook are gluttons for it, being enthusiastic revolutionists, and she had been dreadfully-upset by seeing a policeman killed. She complained of chills and was dressed by the cook in a pair of Huntington's woolen pajamas and put to bed in a hot little mezzanine bedroom up a ladder from the kitchen. There she developed a high fever and violent delirium. H. and I took the case in hand, as the shooting in the streets made it impossible to go for a doctor.

The mezzanine was a perfect oven, so we gently lowered her down the ladder and put her in her own bed. She kept moaning about the dying policeman and a little boy who had laughed; again and again she repeated, "That little boy shouldn't have laughed! It was horrid to laugh!" We got a pan of snow from outside and made an ice-pack for her head. I agreed to hold it on for the first spell while Huntington got a snatch of sleep, but just then she became violent and began tearing the buttons from her garment and putting them into her mouth. I tilted her forward and slapped her on the back till she coughed up the first one; but when she plucked at the second, I lost my nerve and called for help. We finally quieted her by giving her the little enamel ikon which hung on a nail by the bed; this threw her into a religious ecstasy which was touching to behold. She had been muttering *"Tazhaulaya zhisn!"* ("It's a burdensome life!") but now she cooed with pleasure. She finally went to sleep at about three and has lost most of her fever this morning; also most of her hair.

While dressing, we heard a rumor from our intelligence department, Varia the cook, that policemen had opened fire on passers-by from the roof of this building. There were crowds of soldiers everywhere and by peering cautiously through the lace curtains we could safely watch the squads that tramped to and fro in the courtyard; the leaders were in earnest discussion, pointing upward frequently and going first into one entrance and then into another. Hardly had we sat down to breakfast than there was a great tramping in the kitchen and our little dining room was filled with husky Russian soldiers, glistening bayonets and the inevitable acrid smell of boot-leather. I had a vision of a cold walk to the Duma, but the single word *"Amerikantsi"* satisfied them and they swarmed out smiling.

When we left the building they were still on guard and a great throng of them were clustered about the Sergievskaya door. We stopped to watch the proceedings, and presently saw preparations for the warm reception of one of our fellow-tenants. An automobile was stopped, its door opened, and the soldiers formed two lines. One of them clubbed his rifle, another with a drawn sword practised striking an executioner's blow, and we thought blood would be shed. Then in the doorway appeared an old general in full uniform, perfectly imperturbable. He got into the motor, followed by his valet carrying three glittering ceremonial swords. The crowd hooted, objecting to the use of the auto, shouting that he ought to walk; but there was no violence and the motor sped away toward the Duma.

I went to the Embassy with H. and heard the following item of interest: The revolution may be considered a complete success as the whole Petrograd district is in its hands; revolutionary troops have gone out as far as Tsarskoe Selo, Peterhof and Oranienbaum and persuaded the garrisons there to join them and march into town. The Council of the Empire,[1] acting through a committee of its most distinguished men, Guchkoff, Troubetskoi and others, telegraphed the Tsar stating that the present ministry had never had the confidence of the people and prophesying the complete failure of the war, the fall of the dynasty and great misfortune to Russia unless a ministry satisfactory to the people is formed immediately. This sounds pretty radical from that conservative body.

On Monday, the Duma Executive Committee itself initiated the plan of having every factory in the capital and every regiment of the garrison choose delegates to a council which should co-operate in restoring order and establishing a new government. This council was quickly formed, chose as its president Duma Member Chkheidze and as its vice-president Skobeleff and adopted the title "Council of Workmen's and Soldiers' Deputies."

The Revolution deserves its success. It is working out so well that I wonder if it was not all planned beforehand. Everything proceeds in good order; the only confusion today is caused by the last stand of the police and the arrest of all friends of the old regime. There has never been much looting except from government stores. A few food shops which were locked up at the first sign of trouble were broken into, and others with German names suffered. But most provision stores stayed open and did a good business. Now the breadlines are forming in orderly fashion, though without police superintendence, and the market women are patiently waiting as usual, but more contentedly, for they know they are fairly treated. Prices are lower. The soldiers are orderly, too; many exhibit officers' swords, field glasses or equipment, but no other plunder. There are now considerably fewer rifles in civilian hands.

---

[1] Footnote in original: The Council of the Empire is the upper house of the national legislature and one-half its members are appointed by the Tsar. It is the same sort of a death-chamber for legislation as the Bundesrath in Germany.—J. L. H., Jr.

At the Embassy they get all the latest samples from the rumor factories. Here are a few: the hated Protopopoff has been killed by a sailor; the ministers have escaped to Tsarskoe Selo; they are, on the contrary, meeting in the Admiralty under the protection of a loyal regiment; Gen. Ivanoff has been appointed Dictator of the Empire by the Tsar and is marching on the capital with loyal troops.

Dr. Downer, just arrived from Tsarskoe Selo, says that the people of that suburb have not heard of the revolution except as unimportant bread riots. It is rumored there that the Tsar will arrive this afternoon and will come to Petrograd to address the Duma.

Under instructions from the Ambassador, Dr. Huntington was sent off to interview the telephone and telegraph people about service, and I joined him for the three-mile walk across the disturbed districts of the city. The Ambassador wishes to send code messages to the State Department, and to get messages from abroad which may have accumulated during these three days of confusion. The telephone is out of commission because on Monday someone tore the iron cover off the control box on our corner and ripped all the wires loose.

We hear that with few exceptions telephone connections have been preserved, although the operators say, "I won't connect you with any general and if you are a general, I won't give you any connection." Members of the old government receive no service in their homes.

On the Liteiny we saw many groups of people listening to the reading aloud of news bulletins. This is the revolution's way of spreading the news and is very effective in a land where only a small proportion can read. Such gatherings were never allowed before on the streets of Petrograd.

In the Pantaleimonskaya a police station had been badly wrecked and for a block we walked in a black snow-storm of burnt records.

In front of the Engineers Palace we found a company of soldiers drawn up and a great crowd gathered. In the courtyard stood an armored car, and around it a fierce argument raged. Meanwhile soldiers were imperturbably carrying boxes of revolvers out of the palace and piling them nearby. At one time the argument was so hot that one faction had a motor, with two machine guns perched behind, backed up to the archway so as to cover the other faction. But before this and the armored car came to blows a settlement was affected.

We crossed the Mikhailoff Square to the Hotel Europe and Huntington suggested that we stop long enough to reassure some American friends. From their window we witnessed the behind-the-scenes of a street battle. First we heard volleys of shots from the direction of the Nevsky; then we saw armed sailors retreating frantically down the Mikhailovskaya, dodging into doorways, areas and behind all possible cover; one man made the whole distance to the protecting corner of the square at a run with a queer little jerky half-stop in front of each possible shelter. The police must have fired from the roof of the hotel or of the City Hall beyond, for from their hiding-places the sailors began looking and pointing toward a spot on the roof just above the window we occupied. We thought they saw us and stood back out of range of breaking glass. Just then a squad of cavalry and a company of infantry entered the square from a side street, and, thus reinforced, the sailors rallied and all came gingerly over toward the hotel and were lost from view. When Huntington and I went downstairs, they were in possession of the lobby and we had to search out their officer and show our identification letters,[2] written in Russian and signed and sealed by the Ambassador, before we could depart.

That neighborhood and the quarter behind the Kazan Cathedral were the active field of the day's operations. We rounded the Nevsky corner safely, but on all sides heard rifle-shots and machine-gun fire. The west bank of the Moika Canal was a roomier, safer promenade than the Morskaya and, by stopping at each corner and craning down the side-street, we were able to reach St. Isaac's Square without casualties. Once or twice, as we looked up the streets on the other side of the canal, we saw men who seemed to be spraying the buildings indiscriminately with machine guns.

When we got to the Astoria Hotel, we found its first floor a complete wreck. This hotel was commandeered by the old government six months ago and has been used as a luxurious headquarters for the higher officers. The mob had captured it a few hours before we arrived; they had killed some officers, dragged a hiding Roumanian out by the feet, and then had broken everything in sight. The great windows of the ground-floor parlors were jaggedly shattered and gaping, the furniture was grotesquely dismembered and upset, papers, books and even stationery were strewn half-burnt everywhere. The snow of the Morskaya was cumbered with hundreds of broken bottles and soggy with spilt wine. And yet in one room where the furniture was a pile of kindling wood and even the electric brackets had been torn away, we saw large framed photographs of the Tsar, the Tsarina and the Tsarevich hanging on the walls perfectly undisturbed.

The boarding of the main door of the German Embassy had been torn away and that of one of the upper windows, too; so they must have tried their hands there again. This contrasts with the gentle treatment accorded the Austrian Embassy even at a time when it was a refuge for loyalist soldiers.

At the telegraph office we were referred to the Commandant, a very intelligent young lieutenant. No bureaucratic red-tape now! He could find no in-coming cables for the Embassy, but let us look at the receipt book of foreign messages, showing three from Jassy, one from Saloniki, one from Stockholm, and one from Berlin. Of course, said he, we could send messages in code as much as we liked; and any other messages would be promptly cared for. He looked as if he meant it and we felt that a new era had come for Russia. The office was full of busily working clerks and appeared quite normal.

---

[2] Footnote in original: All Americans who applied were given these.

On our return we stopped at the corner of the Synod to see the arrest of an aged civilian-colonel, who was objecting excitedly to a three-mile trip to the Duma on foot. After seeing him safely started we walked through the gardens in front of the Admiralty and looked for traces of a desperate defence; but the great building seemed deserted and as quiet as the grave. We turned down a side-street and watched a business-like civilian commandeer a motor from a very disgusted young lieutenant. The civilian raised his hand to stop the car and said a few words to the officer, who promptly climbed out. The motor was added to a collection in a courtyard, and the lieutenant slunk off unhappily.

The streets are crowded, and now that the miscellaneous firing is limited to a few well-defined districts and the breadlines have begun to occupy so much sidewalk space, people usually walk in the roadways. There are no horse vehicles nor street cars, and while scout automobiles, news-distributing motors, armored cars and armed trucks run pretty fast, there is plenty of room for side-stepping. All these varieties of motors are very picturesque, especially the scout cars full of eager soldiers standing with rifles half levelled, those with machine guns set up in the tonneaux, and the big armored cars.

At the telephone office we had to pass the usual guard of soldiers. They were commanded by a little blond scared-looking officer-boy, who, when he heard we were from the American Embassy, drew us aside and asked in French, very earnestly and pathetically, "Do you think you could get me the necessary papers to go to America?" H. asked why and he answered, "Oh, the situation is getting very bad over here. It's very dangerous and I don't like it at all." Poor youngster, he is probably the scion of some unpopular noble family, just clinging to the Revolution by his eyelids and knowing that a single misstep will end him.

In the telephone office we found everything quite normal. The manager knew about the Embassy's plight from a message previously sent him by courier. He had the index cards for our phone-numbers on his desk and said that a man had already been sent, first to another job on the Nevsky and then to us. He was speaking the truth, we found later, to our amazement. A new day has dawned in Russia when one gets service within 24 hours of application!

On the Nevsky-Morskaya corner, we ran into a regiment preceded by its band, fully officered and in perfect order; the higher officers were mounted. Behind the last file came rank after rank of officers, weaponless and with arms linked; some of them were swathed in bandages and one or two could hardly drag one foot after the other. We could not make out whether they were prisoners or a voluntary part of the parade. Certainly there was no guard around them except a crowd of street boys. At the Morskaya the greater portion of the regiment turned toward St. Isaac's Square but these officers kept straight on toward the Admiralty.

At dinner, the soldiers again visited our apartment. They asked a few questions, succeeded in stealing the cook's alarm clock, and departed. The cook says that these visitants are several things, but specifically that they are the same Cossacks who used to shoot into crowds and to charge them with knouts and with drawn sabres.

Protopopoff, the immediate cause of the Revolution, is a prisoner at the Duma. Goremykin was arrested, too; and Stürmer; and Gen. Sukhomlinoff, the War Minister convicted of selling information to the Germans, imprisoned but released by the late government.

The rest of the ministers have resigned. The good and indifferent ones are left alone, the bad ones confined at the Duma.

Thursday, March 15. Monday, Tuesday and Wednesday were the successive days of the revolt of the troops, the breaking of the resistive power of the old order through the police, and the disappearance of the old government. Logical steps, accomplished quickly, neatly and without much unnecessary bloodshed. Thursday begins reconstruction.

The revolution has not broken the age-long Russian habit of getting up late. Mr. McEnolty went shopping at 8:30 yesterday morning and could buy anything he wanted, for he was the only customer in the shops.

As Huntington and I left the apartment this morning, we met our head *dvornik* (janitor), who has been missing since Monday. This is a great apartment building for generals and such, and the story was abroad that this man was a police spy and that the revolutionists had abolished him. Apparently we had been wronging the poor fellow by our suspicions.

We went down to the Second Division of the Embassy and just beyond the barricade which still blocks the Liteiny, we met as beautiful a body of troops as I ever hope to see, fully officered, fully equipped, with battle-flags bearing sacred pictures. A well-dressed man on the sidewalk told us that this was the Kadetsky Korpus, the Imperial military school, on its way to the Duma to offer its services.

The Ambassador has heard through Mr. McAllister Smith who heard it from a near relative of Rodzianko, that the Tsar has abdicated, the Tsarevich succeeding him with the Tsar's brother, the Grand Duke Michael, as regent. As we were all anxious to confirm this, Huntington and I volunteered to go to the Duma, get in somehow, and interview a member of the Executive Committee or some other functionary who could give us official information.

Before starting, we heard of the death of Gen. Stackelberg, the general who led the forlorn hope to relieve Port Arthur in the Russo-Japanese War. This general was stupid enough to fire his revolver into a crowd of soldiers from the window of his house near the Marble Palace. They took him out on the Quay and when he fell down, trampled him to death.[3]

---

[3] Footnote in original: This story of the death of a gallant soldier is not accurate. He was arrested without warrant, and lost his life because someone fired a random shot which his guard took for an attempt at rescue.

At the Duma we purposely avoided the dense soldier-mob before the main entrance, knowing the hair-trigger temper of its outposts. Instead we went to the comparatively deserted east entrance and presented our identification papers with their great red U.S. seals; the sentinel who could not read but did not want us to know it looked wise and showed us into the office of the chief-of-police. There we again exhibited our papers and were courteously admitted to the main corridor. We pushed through groups and crowds of civilians and squads of soldiers and stepped over the feet of innumerable page-boys who sat on the floor behind the people. Presently we almost collided with President Rodzianko who was striding along the corridor followed by an eager throng. Then we met Mr. Shidlovsky, a member of the Executive Committee, whom Huntington knew. We began to question him, but he was very preoccupied and told us to look around a bit and then to take a chance and drop in at his office in about an hour.

The building was a wild confusion, with every corner occupied. The floor of the main hall was piled high with sacks of flour, crates, bolts of cloth, and all sorts of supplies. Among these piles moved delegations of soldiers from the regiments lined up outside, officers, dignified *chinovniks* in civilian uniforms, eager students in green overcoats and caps. On one side, a group of soldiers was studying the portrait gallery of members of the present Duma, turning rapidly the hinged wooden leaves on which the photographs were mounted and exclaiming gleefully when they found Kerensky, Chkheidze or some other favorite.

We had to show our credentials again to pass through the colonnade into the beautiful Ekaterinsky Hall which is the lobby and promenade of the Duma. In this lofty white-pillared room, several companies of the Kadetsky Korpus were lined up and a thousand or more other soldiers and civilians crowded around them. Every one, except a few readers or arguers on the outskirts, was listening to orators who stood in the low gallery leading to the rear seats of the Duma Chamber. When we entered, an untidy little workman was shouting himself hoarse, emphasising his words with a single gesture like the crawl-stroke of a swimmer. He was crying, "Workingmen, arise! The Revolution is not over but only half done. The laboring people must triumph completely and must rule. It is not right for the Executive Committee of the Duma to sign orders as the equals of the Council of Workmen's and Soldiers' Deputies!" He was interrupted by cries of *"Mozhno! mozhno!"* ("It is permitted!") and forthwith subsided. A big black-bearded fellow with a hooked Jewish nose mounted the rostrum and attacked the war as a thing of financiers and capitalists. Just as he was getting into his stride, the cadet-officer called his men to attention and they marched off, drowning with their cadenced tread the shouts of the orator. The audience showed no sign of resenting this interruption, and greeted with distinct murmurs of disapproval the speaker's further tirades against the war. They applauded vociferously the patriotic sentiments of the earnest soldier who spoke next. Anyone could preach any doctrine to liberated Russia, but radical propaganda was not popular.

At this point men went through the hall distributing the first printed order of the Council of Workmen's Deputies, and we retired into a corner to decipher our copy. It commanded that strict discipline should exist in the ranks of the army, but no subserviency outside of ranks; that the soldiers should drop all titles for officers such as "Excellency" or "High well-born" and use the forms of address "Mr. General," "Mr. Colonel," etc.; that the officers should not treat the men roughly nor address them with the pronoun "thou."[4]

Then we went to Mr. Shidlovsky's office and were admitted without difficulty. Capt. Grenfell, the British naval attaché, was with him. We asked for an exact statement of the situation and Mr. Shidlovsky answered, "Well, we are trying to form a cabinet. We propose to dethrone the Tsar and put his heir on the throne with the next-of-kin as regent." I said, "We have heard that that has already been done." He replied, "Not yet, but that is our programme"; then he added "Of course we are not masters of the situation. The people and the soldiers dominate, so we have to go very carefully." I told him of the socialist speeches outside and asked him if he regarded them as a grave factor. He said he did not; but when we showed him Order No. 1 he studied it, frowning, and said it was bad. He expressed fear that there was great disorder in Petrograd and when we praised the wonderful orderliness of the revolution and the genius it showed, he seemed much pleased. He said, "Of course a majority of the arrests have not been by our order." Here Capt. Grenfell interrupted to ask Mr. S. to sign permits for the admission and provisioning of 40 marines for the protection of the British Embassy, and our interview ended. Mr. Shidlovsky is leader of the Progressist block of the Duma, a rather conservative group, and is much less advanced than Miliukoff and many others of the committee.

We asked Capt. Grenfell what he knew. He said, "The Tsar is at Pskoff under guard. He's not exactly under arrest, they're treating him very nicely and all that sort of thing. But we needn't think of him anymore." We asked about the Ivanoff dictatorship and he said that it was an old move and had come to nothing; there would be no action by the army against the revolution. Just then in came a big broad-shouldered chap of about thirty-five, very agreeable and with a good command of English. Huntington knew him and introduced him to me as Mr. Tereshchenko, a vice-president of the War Industry Committee. He had business with Mr. Shidlovsky, so after a few words with him and a farewell to the latter, we departed.

In the afternoon, I started out with Huntington to the telephone office, to try to speed up the repairing of the still-unresponsive Embassy phone. In front of the *Novoye Vremya* office on the Nevsky-Sadovaya corner, we found a great crowd studying a bulletin board which gave the names of the new cabinet as "approved by the Duma in harmony with the Council of the Workmen's and Soldiers' Deputies." I took down

---

[4] Footnote in original: After the Revolution.—It is now claimed that this order was printed and distributed by German agents.

the list in my notebook, as many others were doing: President of Council of Ministers and Minister of the Interior, Prince Lvoff; Procurator of Holy Synod, V. N. Lvoff; Ways of Communication, N. V. Nekrasoff; Justice, A. F. Kerensky or Maklakoff;[5] Controller of the Empire, I. V. Godneff; Foreign Affairs, P. N. Miliukoff; Trade and Industry, A. I. Konovaloff; Public Instruction, Prof. A. A. Manuiloff; War and temporarily Navy, A. I. Guchkoff; Finance, M. I. Tereshchenko; Lands and Agriculture, A. I. Shingareff.

The names represent the best talent of liberal Russia. Prince Lvoff, the new premier, is not now in either chamber, but is president of the Governing Committee of the All-Russian Zemstvo Union, which for the last two years has done far more than the government to keep Russia in the war; the Union is a great proof that executive and organising ability do exist in this country and its guiding spirit is Prince Lvoff. He seems a remarkably wise choice for the head of the new government. Guchkoff, the war minister, represents Moscow in the upper chamber, the Council of the Empire. He is a wealthy merchant, newspaper-owner and philanthropist, and is president of the War Industry Committee, another of the great private agencies which has been maintaining the war. Prof. Miliukoff's selection for the Foreign Office is excellent too. He knows America and England well and is much in sympathy with western institutions; he is admittedly the greatest Russian authority on the Balkans, having lived in Sofia a number of years and founded in that city the Bulgarian national university. Furthermore, he is the veteran fighter for liberty in Russia and has run the risk of his life over and over again. For a long time he was an outcast in the eyes of the government and it was unsafe for diplomats to know him. Shingareff came to the Duma as an unknown doctor from Little Russia and studied up on finance and agriculture until he was in a position to correct bureaucratic ministers repeatedly on financial and agrarian questions.

Nekrasoff is vice-president of the Municipal Union and a Duma liberal of many years' standing. Prof. Manuiloff is the rector of the great University of Moscow. Tereshchenko (our acquaintance of this morning) comes from Kief and is a great landed proprietor; as second vice-president of the War Industry Committee, he has been the foreign exchange expert of the volunteer business-men's organisation which has taken over the whole management of the munitions supply. Kerensky has been the leader of the little group of Social Revolutionaries in the Duma and an open advocate of terroristic measures. He is a brilliant lawyer but gives much of his time to the free defence of terrorists and "political."

Rodzianko has refused a seat in the new cabinet and continues as president of the Duma.

---

[5] Footnote in original: Apparently there was some doubt at first whether Kerensky should even be included in the ministry.

At the telephone building we found the male employés collected in the courtyard listening to a harangue from an orator on a stepladder. There was hardly a man in the building. Many telephone girls, gathered in the main hall, complained to us that there was no manager to set them to work.

In front of the Hotel France we met Dosch-Fleurot of the *N.Y. World* just back from the Duma, who reported that that body and the Workmen's Deputies had both confirmed the new cabinet. He could give us no news about the abdication of the Emperor.

On the Palace Square we saw a strange sight, a motor with red flags above the headlights and a large British flag fluttering on the running-board.

The Germans had a hand in starting the present disturbance, people say. Bad handling of supplies through Russians of German descent, food shortage, riots, socialist propaganda, hampering of the war, such was their programme; then possibly a revolution as a pretext for the bureaucracy to make a separate peace. What a boomerang it will prove! If the Tsar abdicates, it leaves the Kaiser as the only absolute monarch in Europe.

Today began with a snowstorm, but became beautiful later. We have not heard a shot fired all day.

Friday, March 16. The first action of the new order has been the abolition of capital punishment. In the words of Kerensky, the Revolution "will not resort to the methods of the old regime."

I went to the Embassy early with Huntington and was invited to a "council of war." —— is very pessimistic and says the soldiers who have been in revolt will never be good for anything again, that the revolution will take all the starch out of the troops at the front, and that we can no longer figure Russia as a factor in the war. Granting the demoralisation of the Petrograd regiments, neither the Ambassador nor any of the rest of us can agree to the other conclusions. Seventy thousand men is the maximum of troops involved, and this is a mere drop in the bucket. —— hears that the Germans have made successful advances at both Riga and Dvinsk under cover of the unsteadiness of the Russian armies, and that the English and French are very blue about it. One of those present had heard, on the other hand, that there was a revolution yesterday in Berlin and that the Kaiser was killed.

Whitehouse came in with sanguinary stories. A general was driving peacefully along a main street in an open sleigh, when a shot was fired from some unknown quarter; soldiers blamed the general and slaughtered him. Loyal troops arrived last night at the Baltic Station and were met there by a revolutionary regiment with a bloody battle as a result and much wreckage of property. W.'s brother-in-law, a Finnish officer in the Russian army, was in the Officers' Club shortly after the attack on the building, and in the washroom stumbled over the body of a general and that of a captain, both of which had been overlooked in cleaning up.

W. told us that his brother-in-law and other officers had signed an agreement with the Duma but that when it was published it had been materially changed. They telephoned a complaint to President Rodzianko who sent Purishkevich (conservative deputy from Kursk and reputed slayer of Rasputin) with an apology and a promise to make the necessary correction.

The officers of the garrison have all been obliged to present themselves at the Duma and take an oath of fidelity to the new government; and those who refused have been arrested. Despite the hostility of the enlisted men, now all-powerful, one sees hundreds of officers walking the streets with utmost unconcern.

The rumors of the day are that Stürmer has died of heart-disease; that the Socialists are gaining and have rejected the cabinet they agreed to last night; that the Russian flag has been hauled down and the red flag has replaced it on the Duma; that the Tsarevich is very ill and the royal family will not join the Tsar until the child is better. The Tsar's abdication is still wrapped in uncertainty.

We hear that Protopopoff had all the police organised for defence, rifles and machine-guns planted in convenient places throughout the city and a regular campaign planned. If this is so, it explains the desperate foolishness of the sniping and wild shooting by police agents, the poor dupes thinking that they were playing their parts in a successful suppression of the revolt. When Protopopoff gave himself up, the story runs, he gave to Kerensky a full plan of the defence system; and the soldiers who were sent out found policemen and weapons in practically every place listed. They even found machine-guns in the towers of St. Isaac's Cathedral. Was this betrayal of his agents an honest effort to stop bloodshed or a crafty attempt by Protopopoff to buy himself a little clemency from the powers-that-be?

A very clever Russian, who until recently was minister to China, came in this morning with a story of a truly hair-raising escape. He lives in a house from the roof of which some uncaught lunatic was sniping this morning. Soldiers entered his apartment and found a window open and near it a rifle belonging to his son. They arrested him, tore him away from his wife, and led him off to be shot. At the street-door there was a demonstration and a woman threatened him with a butcher knife; he described the scene as worthy of the French Revolution. He was put on a truck, he said, between a guard of two drunken soldiers but was able to explain his liberal sentiments satisfactorily to an under-officer, to whom he slipped some money, and was allowed to escape.

Huntington and I started out for news and went over to the *Novoye Vremya* editorial rooms. On the way we saw many groups of people who were listening to loud-voiced volunteers reading the news-sheets, but no sign of the inflammatory street-speaking which we all dreaded so much. The possible triumph of the extreme radicals is now the greatest threat to the success of the Revolution.

The headquarters of the *Vremya* are in an obscure side street, but we recognised them afar by the long line of people waiting for bulletins. We went upstairs to the head office where the doorkeeper speedily introduced us to two youthful Suvorins, owners of the *Novoye Vremya* and the *Vechernyeye Vremya*. These papers have always been conservative, sometimes painfully anti-liberal. Now their owners say that the revolution is complete and is a fine thing for Russia. They mention with unconcealed amusement the fact that their political editor, a notorious reactionary, has fled and was seen yesterday in Moscow headed south. They do not expect him to return.

They introduced us to the entire staff and sent out to the reporters' room for the latest news. Meanwhile they told us that the rumor of a split between the Duma and the socialists was untrue and that the socialist parties were in full sympathy with the new ministry. Among the latter, they praised especially Guchkoff as a man of vast ability and firmness.

The Tsar abdicated at Pskoff at three yesterday afternoon. Guchkoff whom he had often described as the most dangerous man in the Empire was the minister charged with procuring his signature to the abdication. Gen. Ruzsky and the deputy Bublikoff accompanied Guchkoff.

They had no news of a German advance at Riga nor of a revolution at Berlin.

Our old friend Shershevsky showed us the galley-proof of the new government's programme. The ministers propose to hold office only until a constitutional convention elected by a universal direct secret ballot can be assembled to determine the future form of government. About this, Shershevsky said to us: "Who knows what it will be? A monarchy is dreadfully expensive. If the Chinese can have a republic, surely we Russians can."

When we returned to the Embassy with our news, we learned of one new phase of the situation. A Mr. Smith had come in to apply for a new passport. Last night a group of men in soldiers' uniforms came to his apartment and demanded to search it. He asked for their authority and they showed a paper which he saw was not genuine; but as they covered both him and his wife with their rifles and were decidedly rough customers, he had to submit. While they were searching, a neighbor's maid came in, and learning the situation escaped before they could stop her. Soon tramping was heard below and the soldiers fled, just as a squad of the new City Militia appeared. The latter denounced the late visitors as released criminals and asked if the Smiths had lost anything. At the time Mr. Smith did not know that the intruders had gotten away with a small hand-bag of his wife's and with a pocket-book containing his passport. So he let the militia go, and later discovered his loss.

The emptying of all the jails has not helped the orderliness of the situation, which however is wonderfully good under the circumstances. A bulletin to householders, issued by the new city government, states that no searches need be permitted unless the searchers show a warrant from the National Duma and that householders may arm for defence and shoot down intruders if necessary.

Pettit arrived from Moscow at noon. He says that the revolution in that city was very quiet, and that he only heard of four deaths: two policemen, an officer, and a civilian. On Tuesday, when the news arrived, one regiment remained loyal and, withdrawing to the Kremlin, prepared to defend itself; but on Wednesday the soldiers thought better of it and gave up without a struggle.

The Tsarevich is reported to have died of measles this morning, that boy has as many lives as old Franz Joseph had.

After luncheon, we saw a socialist procession going up the Sergievskaya toward the Duma, singing the Marseillaise and carrying a banner "Down with the Regency." It was not a very formidable demonstration, not more than three or four hundred forlornities.

Then we stopped to laugh at some clumsy men trying to take down a Romanoff coat-of-arms from above the shop of the apothecary Goldberg; they perched on the roof tree and struggled to detach it from numerous wires and to lower it without breakage. Goldberg evidently thought that he might need it again. The women in a breadline right below smiled as if they knew better.

On the Fourshtadskaya we met Capt. Eames who gave us a budget of interesting news. The Tsar's abdication took the form of placing himself in the hands of the national Duma. The Duma now advocates that as soon as possible there be a nation-wide plebiscite on the basis of universal manhood suffrage, to determine whether there shall be (1) a constitutional monarchy like England, (2) an executive republic like the United States, or (3) a legislative republic like France. This proposition is meeting with great favor among the socialists. A demonstration was called for two o'clock in front of the Circus at the Simeonovskaya and the Fontanka, to protest against the regency; and it resolved itself into a boost for the plebiscite.

Capt. Eames had also heard of bread riots in Berlin and the breaking of windows in the Imperial Palace with a fire-hose.

We went along the Liteiny to the offices of the War Industry Committee; we hoped to find there Huntington's friend Klopitoff, secretary to War Minister Guchkoff, and through him to get from the Minister an official statement of the situation. Klopitoff was not there, but we found a most business-like organisation at work and the offices a hive of industry, just as if revolutionary demonstrations were not passing the windows every few minutes.

Thence we started for the office of the *Bourse Gazette* down in the wharf district of New Holland, about three miles away. On the Nevsky, we passed the *Vremya* office where a single bulletin in each window announced that the Tsar had abdicated. The bulletins in the windows of the *Russkaya Volya*, further down the Nevsky, read: "Nikolai Romanoff has renounced the throne in favor of his son Alexei with the Grand Duke Michael as regent. The Grand Duke Michael has renounced in favor of the people."

On another bulletin appeared the Grand Duke Nikolai Nikolaievich's usual report regarding the Caucasus front addressed not to the Emperor nor to the General Staff, but to the War Committee of the Duma.

All along the Nevsky shopkeepers were removing the double-headed eagles and the Romanoff arms from store-fronts. The ice of the Ekaterinin Canal was covered with the wreckage of these coats-of-arms. We wanted souvenirs but everything we saw was too big.

At the Hotel France we stopped to see Orloff, the manager, and found him wearing the white brassard of the City Militia. This organisation has been formed to take the place of the defunct police-force. It is made up of volunteers, including students, civilians and a few soldiers, and is mustered into companies according to the wards of the city. These amateurs seem to be doing their work with thoroughness and enthusiasm.

We were much impressed to see a great red flag waving over the Winter Palace, and red cloth draped over the double-headed eagles in the scroll-work of the gates.

We found the *Bourse Gazette* people very sceptical about the permanence of the revolution. They had no news except a rumor that Nikolai Nikolaievich was to be restored to full command of all the armies of Russia.

Today has seen the fifth step, the exit of the Romanoffs. On the whole they have gone very gracefully. The Tsarevich is said to have been allowed to reign twenty minutes, before withdrawing in favor of his uncle.[6] The Grand Duke Michael's renunciation of the throne is a typical document of the spirit of this revolution. It reads:

> A grave burden has been laid upon me by the wish of my brother who has transferred to me the Imperial Throne of All the Russias, at a time when we are in the midst of an unprecedented war and uprising of the people.
>
> Inspired, in unison with the whole people, by the thought that above all is the welfare of our fatherland, I have made the difficult decision not to accept the supreme authority unless such is the will of our great people, who must now determine the form of administration and the new fundamental law of the Russian Empire by the popular vote, as expressed through their representatives in a constituent assembly.
>
> Invoking the blessing of God, I beg all citizens of the Russian dominion to submit to the temporary government, risen and clothed with full authority by the initiative of the Imperial Duma; this until such time as a constituent assembly, which shall be called together as soon as possible on the basis of a

universal, direct, equal and secret ballot, can express by its decision the will of the people as to the form of administration.

(Signed) Michael.
Petrograd, March 3 (o.s.) 1917.

I'm going to find out who drafted the above. It doesn't sound like a Romanoff. If Michael did it himself, he is the statesman of the family.

Chapter VII
Reconstruction

Saturday, March 17. Heavy snow this morning and plenty of men out shovelling it. There are many sleighs on the streets, the first we have seen this week, and the appearance of the city is entirely normal except for the lack of street-cars. The Council of Workmen's and Soldiers' Deputies has issued a printed call to the street-car employés for the resumption of service; it draws attention to the removal of the operating-handles from cars at the beginning of the revolution and asks that any patriot having a handle in his possession return it to the Municipal Office. This country has for months been stripped of extra parts for all sorts of machinery, and the removal of these handles was a very effective way to assure discontinuation of traction service when the workingmen wished to paralyse the city and force a crisis.

The programme of the Temporary Government which we saw in proof at the *Vremya* office yesterday consists of the following:

1. Full and immediate amnesty in all political and religious affairs, including terroristic attempts, military insurrection and agrarian crimes.
2. Liberty of word, press, assembly, unions and strikes.
3. Abolition of all class, religious and nationalistic limitations.
4. Immediate preparation to convoke, on the principle of universal, equal, direct and secret suffrage, a Constituent Assembly which will establish the form of administration and constitution.
5. Substitution of national militia for police, with elected leaders and subject to local administrations.
6. Election of local administrations by universal suffrage.
7. The troops taking part in the revolutionary movement are not to be disarmed nor taken away from Petrograd.
8. While maintaining strict military discipline in service, all limitations for soldiers in the enjoyment of public rights as held by other citizens are abolished.

The fact of the war will not be used to delay the carrying out of the above reforms and measures.

Having made itself strong with the obstreperous Petrograd garrison by promulgating the remarkable No. 7, which purchases temporary power at a tremendous cost in future trouble, the new ministry is proceeding in a thorough and effective way to put into force the more enlightened parts of its programme. Most of the Americans in Petrograd are enthusiastic and wish to help the new order in every way possible.

Thanks to me, the United States almost recognised the temporary government this afternoon. I started out to conduct a party consisting of Barry, Platt and Turner to the Duma to pick up the latest news. We went to the east gate as before, and presented our letters of identification to the sentry, who again scanned them long and carefully, especially the seals, and then passed us into the building; Barry had no credentials but we said airily that he was one of our party. Once inside we threaded our way to the Ekaterinsky Hall and persuaded a mystified doorkeeper to admit us to the journalists' room. We recognised no American or British correspondents there and so mounted a staircase to what we supposed was the gallery of the Duma Chamber. Instead we found ourselves on the floor of the Duma, in the midst of a meeting of the Soldiers' Deputies. We only waited long enough to see that it was very animated, so much so that our sudden appearance, like Fra Lippo Lippi's at the Coronation of the Virgin, caused no excitement whatsoever.

Then we sought the lobby and began inquiring for the diplomatic gallery. I addressed several ushers in my best Russian, which was so good that unknown to us they got the idea that we were a delegation of American diplomats come to "recognize" the Duma. We felt that their excitement and the speed with which they led us to the office part of the building were not warranted by the circumstances, but one gets excited very easily these days. Just when we thought we were about to receive season-tickets to the diplomatic gallery, we were shown all unsuspectingly into the anteroom of the President of the Duma. There we were welcomed by a Polish deputy, who luckily spoke French. This simple enthusiastic soul discoursed to us long and eloquently on the great service President Wilson had done for Poland, by recommending Polish independence in his peace message to the Senate. (All the Poles over here feel that way.) Then he said something about getting the President and hurried off.

I was beginning to realise the situation when he came back with a big man of very easy bearing and impressive presence, a calm solid grey-bearded man who made one feel that he commanded the situation. This man reminded me of the glimpse I had had of Rodzianko and I addressed him in French by that name. He replied in perfect English, "I am not Rodzianko. I am large and look something like him but I am Guchkoff." I had nothing ready to say, of course, but was telling him that we were a group of American citizens who were most enthusiastic about the tremendous step forward which Russia was taking, when a breathless boy arrived with the message that the Executive Committee of the Duma would see the American delegation. I immediately said: "M. Guchkoff, we cannot, of course, think of taking up the time of the Executive Committee, proud as we should be to meet that body. We are not a delegation and it is the part of our Ambassador, not of us, to confer with the body which is ruling Russia. Like all Americans, we are keenly interested in the wonderful work of organisation you are doing, and enthusiastic about the liberation of this country, and we have come to watch the process." I think his face fell a little when he heard my first words but he was very cordial and told us that the government was delighted at our interest. He did not seem at all busy or careworn, despite the fact that he is Minister of War and, temporarily, of the Navy. He told us that the Duma was not in session but that the meeting of Soldiers' Deputies in the Assembly Hall might interest us; the main show, however, was the military delegation in front of the building, which he understood Mr. Shidlovsky was addressing. We thanked him heartily and beat a retreat.

Giving up all thought of the diplomatic gallery we went once more into the Duma Hall and stood in an inconspicuous corner behind the seats during one or two speeches. It was an orderly and thoughtful gathering in the main, although some of the soldiers in the back rows were reading papers, sleeping, and paying no attention to the proceedings.

The eagerness of the Minister for American recognition impressed me so much that from the Duma I went straight to the Embassy and told the whole story to the Ambassador and Counsellor Wright.

Our ambassador and counsellor have been the two coolest people in Petrograd this week and the way they have kept themselves informed of all events, have valued all incidents and rumors and have diagnosed the whole situation is a real triumph for the American diplomatic service. The Ambassador's vast political experience gives him better understanding of this popular movement than any other diplomat in Petrograd.

I have been at the Embassy often this week and the entrance has always been unguarded except for the retired negro prize-fighter who acts as doorkeeper. The American flag over the door is enough protection and every one within is tranquil and alert, wholly unhysterical, but quite alive to the world-wide significance of the revolution.

Today for the first time the Military Control has assigned to the Embassy a guard of honor. It consists of seven soldiers, husky good-looking lads from a guard regiment; at least two of them are over six-feet-four in height. Riggs reports that the English and French Embassies each have a guard of twenty-four noblemen's sons from the Corps des Pages. I am willing to back our seven doughboys against any twenty-four pages they can produce.

We hear that the number of dead in Petrograd is only about three hundred. I can well believe this. The killing was almost all one by one. We can find no confirmation of the rumor of group executions or slaughter. The spirit of the governing powers is too clement and that of the people too happy and good-natured, to make these stories probable.

If it had not been for the entire lack of strong liquor, there would have been quite another tale to tell. The situation on Monday had the makings of a French Revolution, and many people here expected momentarily a reign of terror. Vodka unquestionably would have precipitated it.

There is nailed up to-day in every food store an official schedule of the prices which may be charged for provisions, all a few kopecks lower than the pre-revolutionary prices.

Sunday, March 18. We read this morning of the first meeting of the Holy Synod with its new "Ober-Procuror," Mr. Lvoff. The Metropolitan of Kief presided and the attendance was only subject to comment because of the absence of Peterim, Metropolitan of Petrograd, who had refused to accept the new order and had been deposed. The presiding metropolitan expressed great joy at welcoming such a devoted son of the church as Mr. Lvoff. The latter replied that he was glad to be the man to institute the policy of a church absolutely free from political control. He proposed that as a sign of emancipation from mundane domination the Imperial throne be removed from the Synod Hall. This proposal was promptly adopted. It was also agreed that the prayers for the Tsar and the Imperial Family should be struck out of the liturgy.

It is impossible to tell from the newspaper account what the real attitude of the higher clergy was to the formalities of this meeting. The religious spirit of Russia is a tremendous force, but it has been confined in the framework of a paralysed and paralysing political system. If Mr. Lvoff's proposal of complete liberty is carried out and the church divorced from lay politics, it will be one of the great accomplishments of the revolution.

The church services today finished early, for the priests in omitting all reference to the Imperial Family had to cut out a full third of the service. At noon the streets were crowded with a holiday throng. The day was cold and clear and the snow-quilt on the Neva glistened dazzlingly. Up and down above the river wheeled a buzzing aeroplane.

We found that the Liteiny barricade was gone. We examined the ruins of the burnt Law Courts nearby with the idea of getting souvenirs, but the courtyard and passages were filled with Russians who seemed to be far more energetic trophy-hunters than ourselves. Only during the last two days has "collecting" been a safe occupation. Earlier in the week pretty Mrs. D—— stopped before the ruins of a police station to pick up an iron shield half buried in debris, but was greeted with a challenge and turning found herself looking into the rifle of a very determined soldier. She promptly said: "I want to take this back to America as a souvenir of the Great Revolution, to show it to my grandchildren and great-grandchildren when I tell them that I was there when Russia was freed." The soldier grinned broadly and selecting a moujik from the crowd which had gathered ordered him to carry the shield home for her.

After lunch Huntington's doctor, who has an official position with the Nikolaieff R. R. and hence is a government officer, came to examine our convalescing maid. The cook asked him if he could get her some flour. He said that in the days before the revolution he could get all he wanted, but that now he had no inside track. In the old days, there were more grafts than a foreigner could imagine. The police always kept on hand great stores of everything, which they had forced from the shop-keepers, and did a very profitable merchandising business on the side. Government officials could always get their share of the loot.

We went to call upon some apartment-dwellers on the French Quay and found the street-front of our first objective guarded by sailors. We approached the sentry at the front door, who promptly placed the muzzle of a revolver against the fourth button of my overcoat and said something in Russian, which I took to mean that our room was preferable to our company. We retreated with dignity into the crowd and waited until the cordon drove away in a truck. When we entered the building we found other sailors ransacking the apartments of the All-Russian National Club on the third floor.

We heard from the De Wetters, on whom we called, another story of the "battle of Liteinia" last Monday. From the windows of their apartment they saw soldiers take cover under the arched stone railings of the Alexandrovsky Bridge and lie there firing. In the midst of the fusillade a placid old horse-vehicle came rambling out of the Liteiny and jaunted slowly across the bullet-swept bridge as if it were on a country road. This is perfectly in keeping with the popular indifference to rifle-fire which we have seen everywhere.

We also heard from them the tale of the escape of a most courteous policeman usually on duty in front of the French Embassy. Early in the week he slunk into the entrance way of their building in street clothes and begged the Swiss to give him a big overcoat as a disguise, because otherwise the mob would kill him. All the Swiss had to offer was the coat of the D.'s chauffeur; the policeman took this and disappeared, but he left a bank book showing a balance of 120 roubles, to be drawn in payment for the coat if he failed to come back.

A Baltic Russian living in a big apartment building near here saw policemen firing from the roof, and sent a servant to notify the soldiers. When they came, the *dvornik* told them that the policeman story was a lie, but said that there was a German count living upstairs, and directed them to the Balticker's rooms. The policemen were thus given time to escape, while the innocent citizen was led away to the Duma. There a Deputy heard his story and apologised to him profusely. "We know you are all right," said this official, "but we must detain you here an hour, for the crowds are bringing up all the prisoners they take, in the belief that we give them a full trial, and the Duma does not care to dispel the illusion." So the Balticker sat for an hour with a distinguished general and a couple of minor bureaucrats who were in the same predicament and then they were given safe-conducts and sent home.

As soon as people began to realise that arrest by the populace brought with it a guarantee of future safety, hundreds gave themselves up and asked to be arrested. These were mostly bureaucrats of the lower grades who had been honestly doing their best to serve Russia even in that rotten system.

We dined with two American gentlemen at the Hotel Europe. They told us that another American guest of the hotel, a friend of theirs, had on two occasions seen the window through which he was looking shattered by bullets. The Europe stands in the centre of the district which was the last battle-ground of the police.

We also heard an interesting story of prerevolution conditions. An American who had been in Berlin just before the war and knew various members of the German government, was driving down the Nevsky recently and saw in a passing sleigh a man whom he recognised as an employé of the German foreign office. Being quite sure of the identification he went to Police Headquarters and told them about it. They said, "Yes, he is one of four who are here; we know all about them, but we have instructions from higher up to leave them alone."

All automobile owners have received notices from the City Hall that if their motors were commandeered and if they can identify them, they will now receive them back and the City will pay rental for their use as well as a compensation for any damage done. This is surely something new in revolutionary procedure.

Monday, March 20.[1] The Minister of Justice has today declared that he will not continue the legal steps begun against the slayers of Rasputin. The Grand Duke Dmitri Pavlovich and Prince Yussupoff have been notified that they can return to Petrograd without fear.

Prof. B——[2] lunched with us, and as he is one of the ablest men of the new order, we kept him for hours, and got from him many Russian sidelights on the Revolution.

I asked him first how many people had been killed and he replied that there was no definite count but his belief was that there were about a thousand. He knew of few cases where the dead had been very numerous in one place, but said that in a city of 2,000,000 inhabitants a thousand single deaths were quite possible in such a revolution. He confirmed the story about the battle at the Baltic Station; the Anitchkoff Palace was another scene of heavy fighting, as a strong force of police sought refuge there. I have recently passed the palace and its façade is thickly pock-marked with bullet-holes.

Huntington came in and during the greetings B. told us in confidence that he had just been appointed an assistant minister in the new government. He is to be es-

---

[1] Houghteling accidently dated this entry incorrectly. It should be March 19.

[2] Prof. B—— was probably Boris Bakhmeteff, soon to be ambassador to the United States.

pecially charged with American relations, a subject in which the whole cabinet feels the deepest interest.

The ministry desires to open every possible facility for American trade and will impose no more red tape than is absolutely necessary. They are keen for America's interest and understanding. A great new Government Loan in dollars will be negotiated if possible, the proceeds to be put at the disposal of Russian merchants to buy goods in the United States. I told B. that the principal obstacle would be the lack of understanding, on the part of Americans, as to the stability of the revolution and the safety of buying Russian bonds; it would be necessary first to win the confidence of the American people and then such a programme could be on as large a scale as he desired.

This attitude toward us and our trade is a complete change from the petty hampering stand of the late government. If the new order puts through the big internal loan of Free Russia and then can gain the confidence of America and England we will see Russian commerce spring to life and Russia itself leap ahead with tremendous strides.

B. told us of the selection of his friend Tereshchenko as Minister of Finance. The latter has had charge of foreign exchange problems as a vice-president of the War Industry Committee and has done wonderfully well. The Temporary Committee of the Duma did not dare to suggest a banker for the finance ministry for fear of antagonising the socialists and could not find a single revolutionary leader who was a trained economist. So Tereshchenko, who is thirty-three years old, a sugar-beet king from Little Russia and a liberal of very radical tendencies, was selected.

Lvoff, the new Procurator of the Synod, is spoken of by B. as a deeply religious man, much more sincerely so than many of the archbishops. He has fought for years for the removal of lay interference in religious affairs, and has himself been a very active worker in the Orthodox Church. No selection for Procurator could arouse more confidence.

Kerensky, the social revolutionary who is Minister of Justice, is showing up very well. He is clever and fearless and, now that the revolution which was the first article of his political creed has taken place, he is working out the rest of his programme in a way that is reasonable, constructive and humanitarian. When Sukhomlinoff was arrested, the soldiers wanted to kill him, but Kerensky protected him with his own body and outspread arms, saying, "You will have to kill me first!" They insisted then that the shoulder-straps be cut off Sukhomlinoff's uniform, and the minister got scissors and did the job himself. Kerensky is the idol of the people, and everything he does makes him more popular.

Protopopoff the Arch-Bureaucrat surrendered to Kerensky the Socialist, the irony of fate. B. has heard that the fallen minister gave his captor a large map of Petrograd with all the police-hiding places marked on it. He cannot verify the story, but says that the speed with which the police "nests" were found and raided gives color to it. He firmly believes that these police retreats were not designed for defence, but for the attack and slaughtering of the people to cow them and to forestall a revolution.

Some of the members of the late ministry have the sincere respect of their successors. Pekrovsky who held the foreign portfolio is everywhere spoken of as an excellent man and an efficient minister. To him and to Rittich, despite the latter's German name, the Revolution paid the high tribute of not arresting them nor disturbing them in any way. Bark was put temporarily under guard but was not taken from his apartments in the Finance Ministry.

Our guest told us that he had accompanied Guchkoff on a tour of the Caucasus front a few months ago and that the enthusiasm which greeted the latter was tremendous. With his popularity and his technical knowledge gained as president of the War Industry Committee Guchkoff seems an ideal selection for War Minister.

The unofficial organisations like the War Industry Committee, the General Committee of the Zemstvo Union, and the Municipal Union, will now lose the great responsibility which has rested on them through the failure of the bureaucracy; and the great work which they were doing will go on much more easily in the hands of ministers clothed with full power. The bureaucracy took every action it could to hamper them, such as imprisoning the labor members of the War Industry Committee and preventing the Zemstvo Union from holding public meetings.

The proclamation of Grand Duke Michael renouncing the throne was drafted by Shulgin, aided by Miliukoff and Kerensky. Shulgin is a Nationalist, a former conservative and supporter of Stolypin, Miliukoff a Constitutional Democrat and an advanced liberal, Kerensky a Social Laborite of the extreme left. The whole Executive Committee visited the Grand Duke and talked the situation over with him, and the action finally taken was agreed upon unanimously.

According to B., the leaders of the Duma neither expected at this time, nor desired the revolt of the troops; in fact they had been striving to postpone the inevitable uprising until after the war. If the Semenovsky had beaten the Volynians in the Liteiny last Monday, the revolution might have been a failure, the Duma might have been permanently disbanded and the war ended by a separate peace.

The Winter Palace will be reconstructed for the meetings of the Constitutional Convention. Later it will probably be used for the Duma.

Chapter VIII
Order or Chaos?

Tuesday, March 20. P—— went to call on the new Minister of Public Enlightenment today. With twenty people in the anteroom this young American educator was given precedence and had a good ten-minute talk with the minister. Manuiloff said that the first effort of the government in educational lines was to be for primary schooling, to make the people fit for self-government. They will model the system on the American, with all government schools free, but they will not try compulsory education yet. All schools will be open to everyone without distinction of race or creed; he specifically stated that this was to include the Jews.

The street-cars reappeared to-day. The first one came across the Troitsky Bridge from the Petersburg side with a band playing and a great red banner spread aloft: "Land and the Will of the People."

I went to the Hotel France and then along the Nevsky. With the street-cars in operation, everything looked quite normal. There were orderly squads of soldiers tramping to and fro under command of non-commissioned officers, just as before the revolution.

In front of the barracks on the Fourstadskaya, the street was crowded with "awkward squads" of newly-reported recruits, still in civilian clothes; they were being put through foot-drill and squad-formations by snappy, business-like corporals. There was no suggestion of the new freedom either in the discipline or in the attitude of these rookies to their work.

Had tea with Mrs. B. W——.[1] A timorous American came in with a fresh crop of pessimistic rumors. The workmen are refusing to go back to the munition factories. The soldiers are getting surly and are locking up their officers. The socialists are demanding the expulsion of the imperial family and the death sentence on all prisoners of the revolution. A bad revolt has occurred at Kronstadt, with much killing of officers. There has been an uprising at Sevastopol and the whole Black Sea fleet set sail for parts unknown as soon as the news of the Revolution was received. Poor Russia, if one believes some of these fainthearts, she is about done for. We think that she is just beginning.

Wednesday, March 21. W———— of the Embassy tells me on the authority of Tereshchenko that only about 150 of the revolting soldiers and slightly over 250 loyal soldiers and officers were killed in the revolution. The loss of civilians, including policemen, was about 500. Less than a thousand in all, little enough for such a result! The Council of Deputies is planning to have a great funeral for the revolutionary dead in front of the Winter Palace on Friday.

Kerensky has given out an official statement that the socialist demonstration demanding death for the prisoners of the revolution was organised by reactionary agents, in an attempt to upset the nice balance of the present duma socialist entente.

I am one of a number commissioned by the Embassy people to notice whether soldiers are saluting officers and whether the latter are allowed to wear swords. The attitude of the enlisted men toward those of the higher grades has been a menacing factor throughout. In my walks about town today I saw only two soldiers give the salute, but many of the rest had the decency to look the other way when they passed their superiors. We saw three or four of the latter wearing swords, but most were without them.

A courier, just arrived at the Embassy from Stockholm, reports that the Swedish papers printed very lurid articles about the Revolution. There were several accounts, for instance, of the assassination of Sir George Buchanan, the British Ambassador.

Thursday, March 22. H———— says that at a reception last evening he met one of the government censors of newspaper cables. The latter told him that correspondents are now allowed to send any news they wish, except the number of troops in Petrograd or other military information; but that most of them are sending to America the worst slush imaginable.

When I called at the Embassy today to report on saluting and sword-wearing, I met the Ambassador on the stairs, and he said, "You will be glad to know that I have just come from the Foreign Office where I have announced the recognition of our government and made arrangements for a formal meeting with the ministers this afternoon." I expressed the utmost joy. It is a great coup to get in ahead of Russia's allies and it puts the United States in the position of the new government's best friend.

This afternoon the Ambassador and his entire official staff, ten secretaries of embassy and attaches, drove up the Nevsky and through the business centre to the Palace of the Imperial Council; the ambassadorial sleigh was decked with two large American flags and in one of the following sleighs rode the military and naval attaches in the striking uniforms of staff officers. At the palace the entire Council of Ministers was waiting for them. Miliukoff introduced them, and the Ambassador read the cable of the Secretary of State and said a few appropriate words. Prince Lvoff answered most cordially and simply, thanking the United States for this first recognition of the new government. A short informal reception followed. The ministers had all come directly from their offices and wore sack-suits. They appeared careworn but much elated at having won a place among the nations after so few days in office.

We hear that the British, French and Italian Embassies sent to the Foreign Office this morning identical notes of recognition, which arrived only a couple of hours after Ambassador Francis' visit.

Now that the lid is off, the newspapers print the most sensational stories every day. Today there is a particularly lurid account of the efforts of the Tsar to reach Tsarkoe Selo and his masterful consort in the early days of the revolution. His entourage on the special train were mostly drunk, and his chamberlain Voiekoff continued to hide from him the fact that Petrograd was in the hands of his enemies. Finally news reached the train that the army at the front had declared for the revolution, and it suddenly became necessary to tell the Tsar that his reign was over. Apparently he acted in a very manly way, poor little chap. Voiekoff is said to have urged him to open the Minsk front and let in the Germans; the Tsar replied that Rasputin had long ago proposed such a step but that he had always refused.

After dinner we called on the M——s. Here we heard of the treatment of their Swedish maid who was arrested as a spy before the revolution. She was stopped at Torneo, after leaving M.'s service to go home and get married, and was brought back to Petrograd. She was marched on foot on a bitter cold night the entire two miles from the Finland Station to the Secret Police near the Nikolaieff Station. Here she was cross-examined by the judge who is the third-degree specialist of that sinister organisation. His face was artificially whitened, with great blackened lines under the eyes to make him especially devilish, and he raved like a madman and threatened terrible punishments if she did not confess. When she steadily refused she was marched all the way back to the Finland Station and made to spend the night in a chilly waiting-room with soldiers watching her through the glass doors of a warm guard-room. In the morning they led her back exhausted but she kept her nerve even when threatened with death. This same kind of spectacular intimidation was used on her over and over again. Finally the M.'s learned of her arrest, and by exerting influence with various "high personages," they secured her release.

The judge who conducted this inquiry is probably the same man whom A——[2] of the Embassy interviewed about D——[3] some time ago. The judge assumed that the United States wished to disavow D—— and was furious and insulting when he found that he was wrong. D—— says this man told him much "inside information" about the workings of the secret police, saying, "I only tell you these things because you will never leave here alive."

A. hears that this official fled on the first day of the revolution and escaped. M——, on the other hand, is sure that he was torn to pieces by the mob and his body burned on a great fire composed of the records of his office.

Mr. M—— told a story that he had heard from a Swedish manufacturer who was making rifles for the Russian government. These weapons were sorely needed, since many Russian soldiers were going into battle unarmed. But the chief of the arsenal refused again and again to accept delivery, although the rifles had been tested, approved and paid for. Finally the Swede woke up, paid the usual rake-off, and so got the consignment accepted.

The munitions factory connected with the Artillery Arsenal was in full operation when we crossed the Liteiny at about 11:00 P.M.

Friday, March 23. The Council of Workmen's and Soldiers' Deputies seems to be moderating its radicalism. The proclamation that soldiers shall elect their own officers has been explained away by a statement that this does not mean the officers for military matters but those to represent them in certain intra-regimental details. Other rash actions are similarly withdrawn. The plan to bury the revolutionary dead in the Palace Square has been speedily abandoned.

The powers-that-be are still much concerned about the attitude of the radicals but more so about the disorganisation of the army. The Petrograd garrison is quite out of hand, and many soldiers are quitting the front without leave. The War Minister has issued a proclamation predicting a great German advance and trying to rally the army.

We heard today of an American who owns a manufacturing plant in Petrograd and whose factory hands now refuse to work full time. He lost his temper and fired them all but they defied him and would not leave the building. He consulted an influential friend who said, "If I get soldiers to protect your rights, they will join your workmen in making trouble. My advice to you is to eat dirt as quickly and abjectly as possible. You are lucky to have laborers who will work at all."

The American Embassy is swamped with applications from Russian officers who want commissions in the American army.

This evening I started for Moscow. At the station I noticed that the traffic was being controlled by high-school boys of the City Militia and that they showed great confidence, skill and courtesy.

In my compartment were a brigadier-general, a colonel and a captain, all bound for the Caucasus. The captain could talk French, the colonel German, the general only his native Russian. Consequently our conversation was worthy of the day of Pentecost. The general showed me scars where a bullet had entered his skull near the corner of his left eye and gone completely through and out at the back, a most unusual wound to survive; he had also had both arms broken and could only raise them a little way from his sides.

The captain was very agreeable and we had a long and enthusiastic talk about field artillery, his specialty. I asked him how he regarded the disorganisation of the troops in Petrograd and he expressed confidence, saying, *"Cela s'arrangera."* He believes that the revolution will help the war.

A short distance out of the station, a shabby bearded man with a huge bow of red ribbon in his lapel, entered the compartment followed by a squad of soldiers, and made each officer show some sort of a paper. He never even glanced in my direction. When he was gone, I said, "*Qui est ce fonctionnaire-la?*" but the captain replied almost gruffly, "*Je ne sais pas.*"

The corridors of all the cars were full of soldiers. I do not know whether they were going to the Caucasus or taking unauthorised furloughs. They treated my officer friends politely, and I once found my captain talking and laughing with a group of them as if they were old comrades. As he was obviously an aristocrat and a dandy, I was a little surprised at this fraternising.

In a second-class carriage nearby an untidy socialist was arguing against the war and was being heatedly controverted by all present, soldiers, under-officers, students and civilians. Anti-war talk isn't popular.

Saturday, March 24. Lots of freight trains moving now. The transportational paralysis of the pre-revolution period is gone.

Many of the passengers showed great interest in me as an American and went out of their way to show me courtesy. They examined with approval the English-Russian grammar which I was studying. I understand enough Russian to know that there was much conversation about America and Americans.

At our office in Moscow I found very pessimistic about the situation. He spoke despondently of uprisings of peasants and runaway-soldiers in the rural districts and of the looting of country-houses, his own among them. The soldiers believe that the lands of the nobles are to be divided at once, and thousands of them have left the trenches without permission and are raising disorder in the provinces. Gen. Brusiloff has officially taken notice of these absences and has issued a proclamation that all soldiers who are not in their places by April 1 (or April 14, new style) will be severely punished.

The revolution here in Moscow was a spontaneous uprising of the people, almost without violence. A few troops withdrew to the Kremlin and to the Military Garage near the University, but when field guns were trained on the gates of both places they surrendered. This was almost the only excitement and there was hardly a shot fired. The crowds on the streets were immense and people say that the look of exaltation on the faces of the throng was marvellous.

Chapter IX
The Turn Toward Order

Sunday, March 25. This is a great day for the working people, their first full holiday on which they can do what they want without any restriction.

All the servants in this hotel except the floor-waiters are off for the day. Last night the restaurant sent a great variety of cold meats up to our room, to be put on the window-ledges and kept cool for today's luncheon and dinner.[1]

The papers claim that 500,000 people marched in today's Liberty Parade, but my guess is that there were about one-fourth that number. Whichever estimate is right, it was a unique demonstration, vast in extent and wonderfully well-ordered. There did not seem to be any marshals and of course there were no police visible. The crowd along the line of march behaved beautifully, and the groups of marchers kept excellent formation.

Over by the Iberian Gate, Fell and I tried to cross the line of march to go up to the Red Square. We pushed through the lines of spectators and started to make our way between the straggling ranks of a very shabby contingent of workmen. One of them, on the flank toward us, begged earnestly: "Oh, please don't go across; or you'll spoil our order." So we waited. This was the spirit of the crowd, one of conscientious orderliness and of great good-nature. Of course this couldn't have been done but for the prohibition of vodka.

The procession itself was uneventful. There were hundreds after hundreds of groups of soldiers, workingmen and workingwomen, all in like formation, all plodding happily along and occasionally breaking into a modified version of the Marseillaise. This song tells of the liberation of the workingman, and its single verse was sung over and over again with great spirit and a surprising variety of keys; the thin piping of the women's voices at times made it singularly plaintive. The banners carried by the squads were all monotonously alike, red and bearing the inscription, "Land and the Will of the People," or "Welcome Constituent Assembly, Welcome Social-Democratic Labor Party."

Up on the Red Square, we found great crowds of people lining a broad passageway opened diagonally across the centre. As we arrived we heard cheers, and from

---

[1] Footnote in original: Later—The robbers who run the hotel charged us 34 roubles (about $11.00) for these cold meats.

somewhere near St. Vassili's there galloped a squad of about twenty cavalrymen, racing, jeering at one another, and shouting gayly at the people; they reined in at the corner of the Historical Museum, but many of them were carried by their impetus down the hill and almost into the line of march on the Voskresensky Square below. Behind them rode the new military governor and his staff, the former a full-faced, light-moustached, jovial-looking officer, who was hailed with great enthusiasm by the crowds. The staff were all mounted, but close behind them came a procession of automobiles filled with generals and colonels in full uniform. Apparently Moscow feels no hostility to high officers or to military display.

As we returned and approached the line of march in front of the Shrine of the Iberian Virgin, we found the entire column at a halt. The section of red socialists in front of the shrine suddenly struck up a hymn, and every one in the crowd immediately joined soldiers, marchers and spectators, all standing bareheaded in the chilly breeze. It was really rather touching and impressive.

An interesting group in the procession was made up of Sarts from Turkestan. Early in the war there was an uprising of Sarts, Kirghises and Turcomen in Central Asia, which was bloodily put down, and the government seized great squads of these people and sent them as prisoners to various Russian cities. There they were not kept in confinement but were put to cleaning streets, etc. When the revolution came, the Sarts in Moscow revolted, quit work and marched through the city cheering. They were greeted with loud roars of laughter everywhere and are now great favorites.

In front of the National Hotel, there detached itself from the procession a much-appreciated unit. It consisted of a gaudy circus troupe escorting a camel and an elephant, both heavily placarded with the usual revolutionary legends. Behind these came a horse-drawn vehicle bearing aloft a black coffin marked "The Old Order," on top of which perched and grimaced a repulsive little dwarf labelled "Protopopoff." Half the street-boy contingent left the line of march to escort this attraction down the Mokhavaya.

The city authorities and the socialist committees have ordered the soldiers to resume the saluting of their officers. I saw many salutes today. This is a good sign.

I went to tea at the G———s' and learned much news from my interesting hostess and her friends. First I was assured that conditions were gradually righting themselves. Then I heard that the peasants and returned soldiers were plundering country houses, though not burning them. In Moscow, the opening of the prisons has set at large all the dangerous criminals. Some of them broke into the house of a woman neighbor of the G———s a few days ago, terrified the owner into a nervous collapse and made a clean sweep of all valuables. The City Militia are doing their best, but are fairly helpless. Householders are forming associations for mutual protection, with telephone signals for help, etc.

The Moscow revolution had many dramatic qualities. When the city duma declared for the revolution, the Governor-General, who is personally popular with both troops and people, sent soldiers to arrest the whole city government. A young official named Uchensky (?), aged 22, undertook a defence of the City Duma Building, had two machine guns placed at the entrance, organised a defending party and then mounted a horse and went out to meet the Governor-General's troops. He addressed them so eloquently that they came over to the revolution and marched off to demand the submission of his Excellency. The latter said that his oath to the Tsar as a public official prevented his acquiescence in the new order, but for the sake of public quiet he would agree to remain in his house and do nothing. So he was left alone and when the Tsar had abdicated he turned over everything pertaining to his office to the new authorities.

There are only 4,000,000 socialists in all Russia but their organisation is very good and, because of their preponderance among the workingmen in Petrograd and here, they have been able to jump in, claim the credit for the revolution and by dominating the troops usurp the greater part of the power. This power cannot last. The problem is to put them back in their places without bloodshed. Most of them have behaved very well, but there have been extremists, as a matter of course. Some of the unofficial socialist sheets have proposed the abolition of nobility, the free division of the nobles' land among the peasants, etc., and have been very bloodthirsty in tone. The official publications of the socialist parties are moderate and very helpful to the present government.

Kerensky, the Minister of Justice, is the most influential man in Russia today. The responsibilities of office have toned him down and he has become very constructive. He works desperately hard. In the middle of the last week he found time somehow to come down here and direct the Moscow revolution, but after he had addressed a half-dozen crowds on the necessity of a victorious war and the exile of the Romanoffs, he fainted from sheer fatigue. He proposed recently that he should personally conduct the Tsar and his family to England, but in this he was overruled by the socialists, as he has been in several other propositions. The masses are afraid of a counter-revolution if they let the Romanoffs out of their power. Kerensky is a great egotist and talks much about I-did-this and I-did-that; he addressed the Faculty of Laws while he was here and quite disgusted the lawyers by his self-glorification. Still, he needs infinite confidence to carry out the role that has been thrust upon him.

The conversation was led to the probable trial of the Tsar. We talked at great length of the French Revolution, a favorite topic nowadays, and one or other of us pointed out the following features of similarity to the present uprising; the weakness of the monarch, the imperiousness of his consort, the misery of the people, the dissolution of the popular representative body and its refusal to disband, and the moderation of the first popular leaders and of their programme. But the irritants of the

French situation: the emigrés, the invading armies of restoration, the weak trickiness of the king, all causing panic among the people, do not exist here.

Mme. G—— says that the peasants are totally disillusioned about the sanctity of the Tsar, and that a peasant uprising in favor of a monarchy is not likely.

The Workmen's Deputies have ordered that the guarding of the Tsarina be entrusted to them and have forced the ministry to acquiesce. These overrulings of the newly-established government by the socialists are demoralizing; fortunately they do not happen often. The government is wisely very philosophical and long-suffering.

On the other hand, one can easily understand the position of the socialists. They want to accomplish through their own power all they have dreamed of for years, and they must play safe against reaction even if they have to go to extremes. So far the temper of the revolution has not fostered extreme measures, but educated Russians are preparing themselves for any cataclysm.

Someone spoke of the Grand Duke Michael as a decidedly weak man. He is married morganatically to the daughter of a Moscow lawyer, a woman whom the company all knew and characterised as very imperious and shallow, and they have one son.

Guchkoff has a tremendous position in Moscow, but they seem to think that he is gradually losing his popularity in the capital. Still, he made all Russia laugh by proposing in a speech recently that a monument should be erected to Protopopoff, as the real hero of the revolution and the man who made it possible.

As I walked home, I found large street-meetings in session at the Lubyanka Square and in front of the Great Theatre. I could not understand much of the oratory, but most of it seemed thoughtful and unhysterical.

Monday, March 26. A long, quiet day at the office, almost finishing my work. The only excitement was the rumor of a great Russian advance at Minsk, news which none of the evening papers confirmed.

Tuesday, March 27. The soldiers were today ordered by the extremist organisation not to salute their officers, but they disregarded the order.

After lunch I went out with Mrs. S—— to shop for souvenirs. In front of the Trading Row on the Red Square we saw one of the usual "bread-lines," but, strangely enough, it ended at the door of a linen shop. Mrs. S. explained that this shop was supposed to sell extra good cloth at especially low prices; many other dry goods stores in the same building were almost empty, but the Russian women preferred to wait for hours in front of this one in order to save a few kopecks.

In the evening, I went to a party at Vice-Consul MacGowan's. He lives in a building belonging to Nikolas II and in its basements are the great cellars for the Tsar's Crimean wines. The city government sent a guard for this building at the time of the revolution, but the MacGowans trembled lest guard plus wine might be worse than no guard at all.

Wednesday, March 28. The snow is melting fast and drips from all the eaves like rain, and the streets are a sea of slush. There has been a scarcity of men to clear snow since the revolution and the thaw is causing the worst condition Moscow has seen for years. It has been the coldest, most snowy winter in the memory of man.

This morning Mrs. S——, Fell and I went again to the antique shops. We saw many lovely things, but all of them unbelievably dear.

Mrs. S—— complained of the lack of freedom of Free Russia. No paper dares print anything against the present order. There are no courts, no police, no justice. Recently the chauffeur of one of her friends stole a full set of tires and sold them. He was known to be a high-up revolutionist, so his master did not try to have him arrested but paid his wages and dismissed him. He became abusive, announced himself as the revolutionary head of the district, and threatened to cut his employer's throat. Now the family is living in deadly fear.

It will be months before conditions are normal and perhaps more blood must be shed. When one considers the character of the tyranny that was overthrown and the newness of popular freedom, it is a wonder that conditions are not worse.

After luncheon, Fell and I went over to the Tretyakoff Museum to see the pictures. The collection includes some exquisite landscapes, some vivid Cossack pictures, and the famous Vereshchagins, which are a delight to the eye.

Four of us heard Carmen at the Zimina Theatre this evening. The cast was not noteworthy, but the singing was as good as I've heard in that opera. The scenery was most interesting, and the details very clever. The Russians seem to have a great gift along these lines.

Thursday, March 29. Called on A of the Zemstvo Union. He tells me that the choice of Prince Lvoff as premier is regarded as a great tribute to the Union; that the government will now take over the tremendous task which was forced on the voluntary organisations by the incapacity of the bureaucracy and that their work will constantly diminish. He has heard that conditions at the front are better and that the soldiers who left without permission are coming back in large numbers. The great problem is that of ammunition; the workmen in munition factories are very independent and refuse to work steadily or long, the output is far below normal, and the armies are undersupplied. He thinks that the Germans will make a big advance and probably take Riga in the spring unless the labor situation improves, "but," he adds, "we can stop them before they get to Petrograd."

I spoke of the great advantage to Russia in having a full organisation of local self-governments even if they had never had power. He said that of course the *Zemstvos* would be much changed by the widening of the electoral franchise, but that the present leaders hoped to preserve a good part of their efficiency. He pointed out that the tendency would probably be to re-elect the representatives who had made good records in war relief work.

Mr. A—— urged me to work for a better understanding of Russia in America. Especially is it necessary that American Socialists exhort their Russian brothers to be moderate, lest their rashness throw the great victory into the lap of the hated German Imperialism.

In the evening I started for Petrograd. We rode to the station in a wheeled vehicle. The sleighs have been running over bare cobbles all week, and I have seen more and more trucksledges hopelessly stuck each day; but it is still pretty rough going for wheels.

Friday, March 30. Arrived in Petrograd at noon. It is colder here, there is little sign of melting and sleighs are still to be seen everywhere.

Saturday, March 31. Lunched with the W——s.[2] They say that the American recognition, in its priority and its manner, has made the best possible impression on the new government, which now considers the United States its model and its best friend. The Ambassador is being consulted on all sorts of questions, and is undoubtedly doing splendid service to Russia by his level-headed advice.

The W——s say the censorship on all incoming mail has been discontinued.

Sunday, April 1. Graham Taylor came in just after one o'clock. We started for a walk and at the Liteiny ran into a procession of suffragettes, who were marching to the Duma carrying a great banner, "Without the Participation of Women the Electoral Right will not be 'Universal.'" The government is on record for universal suffrage, but the women are afraid that they may be forgotten.

Only a couple of blocks behind came a band followed by a long column of troops. This proved to be the whole Petrograd garrison on parade. All the officers from generals down were in their proper places. Behind the first three regiments rode a stunning group of staff officers, and in their midst General Korniloff, the Military Governor of Petrograd and the hero of the arrest of the Tsarina. Groups of soldiers going upstream to the starting-point kept coming to attention on the sidewalks and saluting him, and he always returned their salutes most genially. As far as we could see, in fact, the relations between officers and men were everywhere cordial and the discipline was perfect. There were no flags except red ones and all of these had devices. There were the old favorites "Land and the Will of the People" and "Welcome Constituent Assembly, Welcome Democratic Republic," but best of all there were hundreds representing a new spirit. One of the most frequent was "Without Victory there is no

---

[2] W——s is likely the Wrights.

Liberty"; then others such as "Victory over Wilhelm and then a free Russia," "Freedom through harmony between officers and men," "We must work with our officers," "First beat German militarism, then a Democratic Republic." We were delighted. This spirit in the Petrograd garrison means the solution of the greatest problem of all. If these soldiers will obey, there will be order in the city and an end of the spirit of superciliousness on the part of the workingmen, which is bolstered up by the feeling that they, instead of the officers, control the soldiers. The reiterated sentiments in favor of the war are reassuring, too.

The parade itself was most impressive. The equipment of the soldiers appeared complete, and their organisation faultless. They were mostly men of fine physique, with only a small proportion of boys and of older men. We watched for an hour but they were still coming, as far as the eye could reach, and on the other side of the street companies of infantry, troops of Cossacks, armored cars, etc., were constantly moving toward the rallying point.

After luncheon Graham and I found the Sergievskaya full of troops. Up toward the Tauride Gardens we saw a squadron of lancers formed in hollow square; and led by curiosity we pushed through the crowd and, forcing our way between the horses, were able to join the foot-soldiers and civilians who were gathered around an automobile inside the square. In the motor stood Rodzianko, President of the Duma, making a speech. When he ended, the wildest enthusiasm prevailed. The soldiers threw their hats in the air and cheered until the horses of the lancers reared and pranced. His motor then moved a half block further, to a point where other foot-soldiers waited in ranks. As soon as it stopped, they surged in around it with great eagerness.

We elbowed our way through the crowd, calculated the distance which the motor would go on its next dash and stationed ourselves accordingly. We guessed accurately, for the auto halted exactly opposite us and we soon found ourselves hemmed in by a thicket of bayonets, not ten yards from the orator himself. The great man's address was clear and direct, and we caught the words, "Victory," "Liberty," "Order," and "Russia" over and over again. His gestures were mostly like a blacksmith's hammer but once he stopped and pointed accusingly straight at us, so that we almost cried out "*Amerikantsi!*" in self-defense. The simple soldiers around us were spell-bound.

At tea, Mrs. W—— told me that she had lunched with some British officers who had seen the parade and who admitted that for the first time they were beginning to feel optimistic about the results of the revolution.

We have heard that at Kronstadt the sailors revolted with much bloodshed, killing 170 officers, including a very efficient and popular admiral who had been put in command at the request of the British. The sailors seem to be responsible for the few excesses of the revolution. In Finland and at Sevastopol they tortured and killed officers.

Monday, April 2. I lunched at the Myedvyed with Bailey and Taylor. The latter told me that he travelled into Central Russia the week before the revolution with a very intelligent and well-informed business man who was managing some oil properties in Turkestan. This man said to him: "We are going to see big things. I will concede the Romanoff dynasty a month but I do not see how it can last longer. Things are rotten beyond repair and the throne is tottering."

At Orenburg the revolution was entirely bloodless. The news of the Petrograd revolt dribbled in and no one believed it at first. When the whole story was known, there was a unanimous celebration led by the governor of the province.

I heard today the details of the wrecking of the Astoria wine-cellars; a friend of mine had the story from the two British officers who were the heroes of the occasion. They lived in the hotel and when they heard that the crowd was approaching to wreck it, they immediately thought of its famous cellars and of the terrible consequences to be expected if the mob got at their contents. So they rushed downstairs and while one of them who talked Russian harangued the astonished wreckers, the other smashed bottles until he was knee-deep in wine. Even then many people carried out bottles but only to have them snatched away and broken by the more level-headed of the wrecking-party. This latter action is the finest tribute I have yet heard to the common sense of a Russian crowd.

Tuesday, April 3. I depart this evening for Siberia, Japan and America. Had an appointment this morning with the Assistant Minister of Trade and Industry at the Ministry on the Vassili Ostroff, and found great difficulty in getting there. The layer of ice on the streets is breaking up fast and conditions are indescribably difficult for horse-vehicles. Since the revolution the drivers of fiacres are all free men and will not go anywhere their sweet fancy doesn't lead them, no matter how much pay one offers. Their charges are arbitrary and terrific. I had a Petrograd business man for interpreter but we found no driver who chanced to harbor a desire to go to the Vassili Ostroff, so we walked a great part of the way.

My interview with the Assistant Minister was purely technical, but after it I asked him, as a matter of curiosity, whether the soldiers knew of the adjournment of the Duma when they revolted on March 12. He said that they did, that they revolted to protect the Duma. My own opinion is that the later regiments probably knew, but that the Volynians and the Preobrajensky revolted because they were unwilling to fire on the people.

I walked home, noticing as I passed the People's House of the Emperor Nikolas II, that the name of the Tsar had been removed from its façade. I crossed the Neva on the ice. On the Quay I saw companies of soldiers with picks and shovels going out to clean the streets.

After luncheon, I went over to say good-bye to Mrs. W———. The wife of the Japanese ambassador was there, a very attractive woman who speaks English beautifully.

She told us that when the Arsenal was taken on Monday morning of the Revolution, a Japanese merchant was in the Artillery Office arranging about a contract, and that in the miscellaneous shooting he was killed. A fellow countryman who was with him brought the news to their Embassy, almost simultaneously with the arrival of a telegram to the effect that a train bringing one of their official commission to Petrograd had been wrecked in Siberia. They conecluded that this was an anti-Japanese uprising and were much agitated. A departure on a Russian railroad is always apt to be hectic, and one cannot be too careful about the baggage that must travel 14,000 miles and pass through five custom-houses in one's company. So I surrendered my last hour of Petrograd to the interesting confusion of the Nikolaieff Station; which no revolution can make less interesting or less confused.

Easter Day, April 8, 1917. In Petrograd there is one Easter story which the old aristocracy loved to tell. It had to do with the Russian custom of kissing the first person one greets after the midnight chimes have sounded on Easter morning. It seems that just before midnight, one Easter eve, Nikolas II was walking in his garden and as the hour struck found himself face to face with a sentry. The good Tsar unhesitatingly said "Christ is risen" and kissed the man.

This morning, on the lawn of a way-station in middle Siberia, we saw a signboard with the proclamation of the local Council of Workmen's and Soldiers' Deputies. It read: *"Spokoistvye i Trud Garanty Svobody"* "Quietness and Industry are the Guarantees of Liberty."

In which of the two, in these simple words of a simple people, or in the kiss and exclamation of the Tsar, is the truer promise of a resurrection?

INDEX

Admiralty, 14, 20, 58, 65, 67
Adrianoff, S. A., 61
Afanasieff, Capt., 17
Afanasieff, Mme., 18
Aleksandra, Empress, xi
Alexander II, 7, 23
Alexander III, 19
Alexeieff, Gregory, 19, 31, 49
America (Americans), viii–xix, 5, 16, 17, 21, 24, 25, 28–33, 35
American Embassy (US Embassy), vii, viii, x, xix, 12, 13, 16, 20, 21, 23, 27, 35, 39, 40, 43, 45, 65, 67, 79, 80, 81, 83, 84, 85, 89, 90, 96, 98
Anitchkoff Palace, 13, 83
Arc de Triomphe, 20
Arctic Circle, 11
Armour, Norman, 12–14, 16, 20, 42
Arsenal, 44, 55, 89, 99
Astoria Hotel, 66, 98
Associated Press, 43
Austria (Austrian), 32, 43, 66
Austro-Hungarian, viii

Bailey, 12–14, 98
Bakeman, Mr., 35
Bakhmeteff, Boris, 83
Balk, Major-General, 56
Baltic Station, 72, 83
Barry, Griffin, 34, 35, 79
Bashlik, 11
Belgians, 20, 26, 31, 35
Berlin, 21, 60, 72, 74, 75, 83
Bogasheff, S. B., 56
Bogolyuboff, Prince Andrei, 36
Bolshevik (Bolsheviki), vii, 9
Bolshoy Prospekt, 14
Bourse Gazette, 48, 75, 76
Borisoff, I. P., 56
Brusiloff, General, 19, 28, 33, 50, 90

Carnes, Mr., 35
Cathedral of the Redeemer, 37
Caucasus, 33, 76, 85, 89, 90
Champs-Élysées, 20
Charity Bazaar, 30
Constitutional Democrat (Kadet), ix, 85
Chicago, viii, 12, 23
Chicago, University of, xix, 31
Chinovnik, 27, 69
Chkheidze, N. S., 51, 52, 64, 69
City Militia, 57, 58, 62, 74, 76, 89, 92
Cold War, vii
Committee of Petrograd Journalists, 48, 60
Constantinople, 36
Constituent Assembly, 76, 78, 91, 96
Copenhagen, 21
Corps des Pages, 80
Cossacks, 19, 31, 32, 39, 40, 41, 44, 47, 60, 68, 95, 97
Council of Deputies, 87
Council of Ministers, 49, 53, 71, 87
Council of the Empire, 8, 52, 56, 64, 71
Council of Workmen's Deputies, 53, 54, 69, 70, 72, 78, 89
Cyril Vladimirovich, Grand Duke, 59

Daily News (London), 17
Delano, Laura, viii
Demidoff, 13
Dewey, Admiral, 12
Dmitri Pavlovich, Grand Duke, 16, 26, 83
Dmitriukoff, I. I., 52
Dobrovolsky, Ex-Minister of Justice, 59
Donan's Restaurant, 20, 21
Dosch-Fleurot, Arno, 26, 72
Dubrovin, Dr., 59
Duma. *See* Imperial Duma
Duma Chamber, 69, 79
Dvinsk, 72
Dvorniks, 46, 68, 82

Index

Eames, Capt., 75
Eastern Front, xi
Ekaterinsky Hall, 55, 69, 79
Engelhardt, B. A., 55

Father Abraham, 46
Finland, 12, 97
Finland Station, 56, 88
First World War (Great War), vii, 7
Flack, Mr., 35
Fontanka Canal, 41, 75
Foreign Office, 13, 21, 71, 83, 87, 88
Fourshtadskaya Prospekt, 21, 41, 42, 46, 75
France (French), 11, 16, 17, 23, 30, 36, 43, 67, 72, 73, 75, 76, 79–82, 88, 89, 93, 94
French Revolution, 73, 93
Francis, David, x, 5, 88

Gendarme Corps, 61
Gerard, Ambassador, 21
Germany (German), vii, xi, xii, 12, 13, 14, 16, 17, 18, 19, 20, 21, 25, 26, 28, 34, 35, 37, 64, 66, 70, 72, 74, 82, 83, 85, 89, 96, 97
Girse, Admiral, 56
Godneff, I. V., 71
Golitzin, Premier, 27, 53
Grenfell, Capt., 17, 70
Grensky, P. P., 61
Guard Equipage, 59, 60
Guchkov, Aleksandr Ivanovich, viii, 19

Hamilton, Mr., 32, 35, 41
Harper, Samuel V., viii, ix, xix, 5, 31
Hermitage, 12, 43
Hermitage Restaurant, 23, 33
Hermogen, 26
Hessian, 33
Historical Museum, 92
Holy Gate, 24, 36
Hotel Europe, 65, 83
Hotel France, 43, 72, 76, 86
Houghteling, Jr., James L., vii–xii, 1, 5, 83
Huntington, Dr., 17, 27, 40, 42, 43, 49, 63, 65, 66, 68, 69, 70, 72, 73, 75, 82, 83

Iberian Gate, 24, 91
Iliodor, 26

Imperial Duma (Duma), 7, 8, 17, 19, 25, 26, 27, 32, 33, 38, 43, 44, 46, 47, 48, 49, 50, 51, 52, 53, 54–61, 63, 64, 65, 67–76, 79, 80, 82, 84, 85, 87, 93, 96, 97, 98
Intelligentsia, 7, 32
International Harvester Company, 24, 26
Ivanoff, Gen., 65, 70
Ivan Veliki's Tower, 35, 36
Ivoshchik, 12
Izmailovsky Regiment, 58

Japan (Japanese), 98, 99
Janissaries, 32
Jassy, 66
Jews (Jewish), 46, 69, 86
Jinghis Khan, 36

Kadetsky Korpus, 68, 69
Kaiser, xii, 13, 16, 72
Karauloff, M. A., 52, 60, 61
Kartseff, Vice-Admiral, 56
Kazan, 34
Kazan Cathedral, 13, 34, 66
Keksholmsky Regiment, 49
Kerensky, Alexander F., 8, 51, 52, 54, 58, 69, 71, 72, 73, 84, 87, 93
Kharkoff, 26, 59, 61
Kief (Kyiv), 36, 61, 71, 81
Kirghises, 92
Kirochnaya Prospekt, 40, 41
Kitaigorod, 36
Klimovich, Gen., 59
Komisaroff, M. C., 56
Konovaloff, A. I., 51, 71
Korniloff, General Lavr, x, 96
Krasnaya Karta, 30
Kremlin, 24, 35, 36, 37, 75, 90
Kriger-Voinovsky, Ex-Minister of Ways of Communication, 59
Krizanovski, M. A., 57
Kronstadt, 86, 97
Kurloff, P. G., 56
Kursk, 73
Kuznetsky Most, 34

Lewis, Mr., 35
Liberty Parade, ix, 91
Liteiny Prospekt, 12, 14, 22, 39, 41, 42, 45, 65, 68, 75, 81, 82, 85, 89, 96

Index

Lithuania (Lithuanians), 17, 23, 24, 25
Litovsky Regiment, 49, 52
Lockhart, Mrs., 34
Lovyagin, A. M., 61
Lubyanka, 36, 94
Lvoff, V. N., 52, 71, 81, 84, 87, 95
Lysogorsky, Assistant Chief, 59

Makavaeff, General, 56
Maklakoff, V. A., 59, 71
Manuiloff, A. A., 71, 86
Marble Palace, 68
Marinsky Theatre, 14, 16
Marseillaise, 43, 45, 75
Marsovo Pole (Field of Mars), 12, 43
Matusoff, General, 52
McClelland, Mr., 21, 43
McEnolty, Mr., 68
McGowan, Mrs., 30, 35
Miliukoff (Miliukov), Pavel Nikolaievich, ix, 8, 17, 19, 25, 52, 54, 56, 70, 71, 85, 87
Milner, Lord, 27, 29
Minister of Provisions, 38
Minister of Public Enlightenment, xi, 56, 86
Ministry of Ways and Communication, 56
Minsk, 88, 94
Moika Canal, 16, 17, 66
Mongols, 23, 29
Monomakh, Vladimir, 36
Moscow, viii, x, 5, 13, 17, 23, 24, 25, 26, 27, 29, 31, 34, 36, 37, 39, 57, 59, 71, 74, 75, 89, 90, 92, 93, 94, 95
Moscow City Railway, 23
Moskva River, 25
Moujik, 13, 82
Municipal Union, 37, 71, 85
Myedveyd Hotel, 41

Narushevich, Mr., 23
National Hotel, 23, 92
Nekrasoff, N. V., 51, 71
Neva River, 14, 81, 98
Nevsky Prospekt, 13, 32, 39, 40, 41, 65, 66, 67, 70, 75, 76, 83, 86, 87
Nikolai Nikolaievich, Grand Duke, 33, 76
Nikolaieff Station, 13, 34, 88, 99
Nikolas II, 14, 94, 98, 99
Novoye Vremya, 20, 48, 70, 73, 74

Oranienbaum, 64

Palace Square, 12, 14, 20, 43, 72
Palmyra Hotel, 21
Paris, 13
Paxita, 14
Peter and Paul Cathedral, 21
Peter and Paul Fortress, 8, 14, 43, 53, 55
Peterhof, 64
Peter the Great, 32, 41
Pettit, Mr., 35, 75
Petrograd, vii–xii, 5, 11, 12, 13, 14, 16, 17, 21, 23, 25, 26, 27, 31, 32, 34, 38, 39, 42, 44, 48, 51, 54–62, 64, 65, 70, 72, 77–81, 83, 84, 87, 88, 89, 93, 95, 96, 97, 98, 99
Petrograd Telegraph Agency, 61
Petropavlovsk Fortress, 21
Piatt, Philip, 23–26
Pikovaya Dama, 35
Pogrom, 37
Poland (Polish), 8, 17, 32, 79
Polski Restaurant, 35
Popoff II, 57
Port Arthur, 68
Praga Restaurant, 24
Preobrajensky Regiment, 45, 49, 55, 56, 98
Prince, Eugene, 17, 28, 34
Procurator of the Holy Synod, 71, 84
Protopopoff, 8, 17, 19, 27, 53, 56, 58, 65, 68, 73, 84, 92, 94
Provisional Government (Temporary Government), ix, xi, 45, 76, 78, 79
Pskoff, 70, 74
Purishkevich, 16, 33, 73

Quay, 14, 37, 43, 68, 82, 98

Randolph, Mr., 29, 32
Rasputin, Grigorii, 16, 19, 27, 33, 72, 83, 88
Red Cross, 17, 35
Red Gates, 29, 30
Red Square, 24, 91, 94
Rein, G. E., 56
Resurrection Church, 23
Riga, 72, 74, 95
Rjevsky, V. A., 52
Rodzianko, M. V., 25, 27, 44, 49, 50, 51, 53, 54, 56, 59, 60, 68, 69, 71, 73, 79, 97
Romanoff (Romanov), ix, 36, 75, 76, 77, 98

Roumania (Roumanian), 11, 13, 14, 18
Russkaya Volya, 48, 75
Russian-American Chamber of Commerce, 39
Russian Revolution, vii, ix, xii, xix, 5–9
Russo-Japanese War, 68
Ruzsky, General, 19, 50, 74

Saloniki, 66
Sapper Regiment, 49
Saratoff (Saratov), 26, 61
Sarts, 29, 92
Savoy Theatre, 30
Second Division, 43, 45, 68
Self-Government of Russia, 31
Semenovsky Regiment, 40, 42, 44, 85
Sergievskaya Prospekt, 13, 21, 40, 41, 45, 64, 75, 97
Sevastopol, 86, 97
Shcheglovitoff, I. G., 52, 56
Shershevsky, 20, 74
Shidlovsky, S. I., 17, 52, 69, 70, 80
Shingareff, A. I., 71
Shirinsky Shaklmiatoff, Mr., 56
Shpalernaya Prospekt, 46, 47
Shulgin, V. V., 52, 85
Siberia (Siberian), 9, 35, 57, 98, 99
Skobeleff, A. I., 51, 64
Smith, McAllister, 30, 68, 74
Social Democrats, 8
Social Revolutionaries, 8, 71
St. Isaac's Cathedral, 17, 20, 73
St. Isaac's Square, 66, 67
Stackelberg, Gen., 68
Stockholm, 11, 26, 66, 87
Stolypin, Peter, 85
Stroukoff, Gen., 44
Stürmer, B. V., 8, 19, 25, 56, 68, 73
Sukhomlinoff, Gen., 68, 84
Summer Garden, 12
Summers, Maddin, 5, 35
Summers, Mrs., 35
Sweden (Swedish, Swedes), 11, 12, 26, 35, 87, 88
Switzerland (Swiss), 21, 82
Synod Hall, 81

Tartar (Tatar), 26
Tauride Palace, 46, 51, 52, 55, 56, 58, 61

Taylor, Graham, 13, 17, 20, 29, 32, 35, 96, 98
Tereshchenko, M. I., 70, 71, 84, 87
Torneo, 12, 88
Traktir, 21
Tretyakoff Museum, 37, 95
Trissell, Mr., 40
Troitsky Bridge, 14, 43, 86
Tsar (tsarist), ix, xi, xii, 7, 8, 19, 23, 24, 25, 26, 27, 28, 33, 49, 50, 64, 65, 66, 68, 70, 72, 73, 74, 75, 76, 81, 88, 93, 94, 98, 99
Tsarevich, 66, 68, 73, 75, 76
Tsarina, ix, 27, 28, 29, 53, 56, 66, 94, 96
Tsarskoe Selo, 27, 56, 61, 64, 65
Turkestan, 92, 98
Turner, Mr., 41, 46, 79
Tyrkova-Williams (Mrs. Williams), Ariadna, viii, ix, 16

Ugreshchi, Nikolai, 25
United States. *See* America
Utro Rossi, 29

Varia (cook), 44, 63
Varkala, Mr., 23
Varvarka Gate, 36
Vassili Ostroff, 14, 98
Vechernyeye Vremya, 74
Vendoff, Lieut. Gen., 59
Vladivostok, 27
Voiekoff, Mr., 88
Voskresensky Square, 40, 41, 43, 46, 92
Volynian Life Guards, 41, 44, 49

War and Peace, 35
War Industry Committee, 8, 31, 52, 70, 71, 75, 84, 85
Warsaw, 28
Washington, D.C., ix, xii
Whiffen, Mr., 43
Whitehouse, Edwin Sheldon, 21, 72
Wilson, President Woodrow, 79
Williams, Harold, viii, ix, 16, 17
Winter Palace, ix, 12, 20, 43, 62, 76, 85, 87
Wright, Joshua Butler, vii, viii, 80

Yussupoff, Prince, 16, 83

Zabelin, General, 56
Zemstvo Union (Zemstvos), 8–9,
    19, 29, 31, 71, 85, 95
Zimina Theatre, 95

Americans in Revolutionary Russia

Vol. 1
Albert Rhys Williams, *Through the Russian Revolution*, edited by William Benton Whisenhunt (2016)

Vol. 2
Princess Julia Cantacuzène, Countess Spéransky, née Grant, *Russian People: Revolutionary Recollections*, edited by Norman E. Saul (2016)

Vol. 3
Ernest Poole, *The Village: Russian Impressions*, edited by Norman E. Saul (2017)

Vol. 4
John Reed, *Ten Days That Shook the World*, edited by William Benton Whisenhunt (2017)

Vol. 5
Louise Bryant, *Six Red Months in Russia*, edited by Lee A. Farrow (2017)

Vol. 6
Edward Alsworth Ross, *Russia in Upheaval*, edited by Rex A. Wade (2017)

Vol. 7
Donald Thompson, *Donald Thompson in Russia*, edited by David H. Mould (2017)

Vol. 8
Arthur Bullard, *The Russian Pendulum: Autocracy   Democracy   Bolshevism*, edited by David W. McFadden (2019)

Vol. 9
David Francis, *Russia from the American Embassy*, edited by Vladimir V. Noskov (2019)

Vol. 10
Pauline S. Crosley, *Intimate Letters from Petrograd*, edited by Lee A. Farrow (2019)

Vol. 11
> Madeleine Z. Doty, *"The Bolshevik Revolution Had Descended on Me": Madeleine Z. Doty's Russian Revolution*, edited by Julia L. Mickenberg (2019)

Vol. 12
> *John R. Mott, the American YMCA, and Revolutionary Russia*, edited by Matthew Lee Miller (2020)

Vol. 13
> Carl W. Ackerman, *Trailing the Bolsheviki: Twelve Thousand Miles with the Allies in Siberia*, edited by Ivan Kurilla (2020)

Vol. 14
> Charles Edward Russell, *Unchained Russia*, edited by Rex A. Wade (2021)

Vol. 15
> James L. Houghteling, Jr., *A Diary of the Russian Revolution*, edited by David S. Foglesong (2022)

Series General Editors: Norman E. Saul and William Benton Whisenhunt